"Every business leader is looking for ways to increase revenue in challenging times. Jeff's new book is filled with short, sweet, fundamental ideas you can put into practice today. Follow Jeff's lead!"

—Gary E. Hoover, Founder, Hoover's Inc.
and Author, *Hoover's Vision*

"A practical, commonsense guide to growing your business. Written with Blackman's usual clarity and humor, it's educational and fun to read. You'll see results and increased profits!"

—Susan RoAne, Author, *How to Work a Room*®,
The Secrets of Savvy Networking, and *RoAne's Rules:
How to Make the RIGHT Impression*

"Loaded with how-to, do-it-now strategies to accelerate your sales."

—Jack Wilson, President, JWA Video

"*Stop Whining! Start Selling!* has all the right ingredients and substance for success. Its focus is on positive selling and marketing skills everyone needs to adopt. It'll help you get the results you're looking for."

—Phil Kuhn, Vice President, Correspondent Lending,
Principal Residential Mortgage, Inc.

"Jeff's insights are invaluable. He removes complexity from the sales process to help you surpass your potential. His wisdom will inspire you to tap your talent and become exceptional, personally and professionally."

—Roz Usheroff, Author, *Customize Your Career:
How to Develop Winning Strategies to Move
Up, Move Ahead, or Move On*

"Real-life solutions for real-life situations."

—Ron Springer, President, Esprit Productions

"Like a meteoric game-winning home run, Jeff's strategies elevate you to new heights of success!"

—Wayne Messmer, Anthem Soloist
and Public Address Announcer, Chicago Cubs

What Business Leaders Say about *Stop Whining!*

"This book is jammed with fast-acting, no-nonsense strategies and techniques you can use immediately to increase your sales!"

—Brian Tracy, Author, *Goals!*

"If you're ready to be immensely successful and profitable and to sell more in less time than you ever believed possible, buy this book now."

—Mark Victor Hansen, Co-creator, #1 *New York Times*
best-selling series *Chicken Soup for the Soul*®
and Co-author, *The One Minute Millionaire*

"If you want proven, creative, and real-world business solutions, here they are. Jeff has written a timeless source for success."

—Denis Waitley, Author/Speaker

"Jeff helped us double sales! His powerful and profitable upgrades led to explosive results, with less effort."

—Bob Williams, President, Burns Sports & Celebrities

"In this book, Jeff provides no-nonsense strategies to succeed in the real world. You'll love it!"

—Mac Anderson, Founder, Successories

"My gross income increased by 30%, and a big part of that was from asking better questions. Be a sponge and soak up all of Jeff's stuff! I did and now have increased income and personal time."

—Brad Wuertz, Financial Associate,
Thrivent Financial for Lutherans

"We are seeing production and profitability volumes we've never seen before."

—Jodi Cornish, Site Manager,
Principal Residential Mortgage

"Jeff opens new doors to success. He shows you how honesty, knowledge, skills, and execution will take you further than you ever thought possible."

—Ed Walovitch, Regional Sales Director, PeopleSoft

"In today's turbulent economy, even the toughest sales professional can find himself looking for new ideas to break through to success. Once again, Jeff delivers just the right message in his uniquely upbeat and conversational style. Whether you're looking to reenergize a stagnant career, motivate new recruits, or simply hone your own competitive edge, Jeff's insights, ideas, and challenges are right on the money!"

—Lori Buss Stillman, Vice President,
Business Development, A. C. Nielsen

"This is the most practical and substantive sales book anywhere. Jeff is an extraordinary teacher. Read this book to learn—to apply its wisdom, to succeed, and to outperform in today's marketplace."

—Nido Qubein, Chairman, Great Harvest Bread Co.
and Founder, National Speakers Association Foundation

"Bite-sized ideas that deliver big-time results! Jeff provides clear, on-target revenue-generating strategies. Buy this book NOW and hope your competitor hasn't bought it first."

—Dr. Tony Alessandra, Author, *The Platinum Rule*
and *Non-Manipulative Selling*

"Learn new strategies to provide value, build your business, and achieve new levels of prosperity."

—Alan Weiss, Ph.D., Author, *Million Dollar Consulting*

"Jeff shows you how to quickly, ethically, and dramatically increase revenues, profits, and earnings. This book is loaded with entertaining and valuable lessons about life and business. It's a must-read!"

—Mike Walsh, President, High Performers International

"This is more than just a book about business success; it's about life achievement. It'll help you fly to that next level with a clear direction and a renewed energy."

—Russ Vandenburg, President and CEO,
EPT Management Company

"We are all *selling* every day, in either our personal or business lives. Jeff tells us how to successfully accomplish this in his powerful new book."

—Al Golin, Founder and Chairman,
Golin/Harris International

"There's lots to learn from Jeff's insights, analysis, and strategies. And he delivers it with humor and good sense. His message filters through our company each and every day."

—Rochelle M. Jacobson, President, N. Merfish Supply

"If you're serious about achievement and growth, then devour this book. Jeff delivers the right focus on both life and business."

—Jeff Liesener, President, The High Achievers Network

"A concise and power-packed blueprint for maximizing your skills, attitude, behavior, and results."

—Jim Elsener, Publisher, *The Business Ledger*

"You hold in your hands . . . a new resource for proven results!"

If you're a:

Rainmaker

☆ Salesperson.

☆ Account executive.

☆ Director of business development.

☆ Account manager.

Leader

☆ CEO.

☆ President.

☆ Owner/entrepreneur.

☆ Vice president of sales.

☆ Vice president of marketing.

☆ Sales manager.

☆ Market manager.

Executive

☆ Association executive.

☆ Director of training.

☆ Sales and technical support.

☆ Director of human resources.

Or anyone who wants others to say "yes" . . .

Then get ready to turn you and your company into a profit powerhouse!

Grow your business
and skyrocket your success as you . . .

☆ Increase sales dramatically.

☆ Enhance profits.

☆ Boost your earnings.

☆ Discover, then execute breakthrough opportunities.

☆ Cement customer relationships.

You'll learn powerful strategies on . . .

☆ Ethics

☆ Sales

☆ Marketing

☆ Negotiations

☆ Customer service

☆ Change

☆ Prospecting

☆ Referrals

☆ Creativity

☆ Time management

☆ Goal achievement

☆ And more . . .

Your journey to explosive new results,
begins now . . .

Stop Whining! Start Selling!

Profit-Producing Strategies for Explosive Sales Results

JEFF BLACKMAN

WILEY

John Wiley & Sons, Inc.

Published by John Wiley & Sons, Inc., Hoboken, New Jersey.
Published simultaneously in Canada.

For general information on our other products and services, please contact our Customer Care Department within the United States at (800)762-2974, outside the United States at (317)572-3993 or fax (317)572-4002.

Wiley also publishes its books in a variety of electronic formats. Some content that appears in print may not be available in electronic books. For more information about Wiley products, visit our web site at www.wiley.com.

Library of Congress Cataloging-in-Publication Data:
Blackman, Jeff, 1956–
    Stop Whining! Start Selling! : Profit-Producing Strategies for Explosive Sales
  Results / Jeff Blackman.
        p.   cm.
Includes index.
    ISBN 0-471-46363-9 (CLOTH : alk. paper)
    1. Selling.   2. Success in business.   3. Entrepreneurship.   I.   Title.
HF5438.25.B545   2003
658.85—dc22   2003016119

Printed in the United States of America.

10 9 8 7 6 5 4 3 2 1

Contents

PROFIT PILLAR III
Winning Words & Wallet Wisdom   71

Profit Points:

PROFIT PILLAR IV
A Profit Parade   115

Profit Points:

PROFIT PILLAR V
Communicate & Conquer 145

Profit Points:

PROFIT PILLAR VI
Referrals: Your Road to Results! 185

Profit Points:

PROFIT PILLAR IX
Fly like an Eagle!   305

Profit Points:

FINAL STUFF   327

Introduction:
Let the Crusade Begin!

Four words will soon change the way the world sells, markets, and does business. They'll be the new mantra of momentum. The words of wisdom and wealth. The phrase that pays.

They'll be sweeping across continents, boardrooms, and sales floors. Business owners, CEOs, entrepreneurs, and sales leaders will soon politely push, urge, and cajole their troops or even themselves to:

STOP WHINING!
START SELLING!

Ain't no time for bellyaching. Moaning. Groaning. Complaining. Or finger-pointing.

How will your success be defined?
With quantifiable goals and measurable results!

Whether you're a rookie or a seasoned veteran, you'll soon learn:

☆ Excuse-eliminating,
☆ Gripe-removing,
☆ Profit-producing,
☆ Surefire,
☆ Guaranteed,
☆ No-holds-barred strategies to . . .

Drive explosive results, make more money, and
achieve greater happiness—starting *now*!

Today's business problems can no longer be solved by yesterday's solutions! So, after 20-plus years of testing, research, development, and application, I've created a series of easy-to-implement business-growth strategies to help you and any size company generate results!

Quickly. Ethically. Dramatically.
Increased revenues! Increased profits! Increased earnings!
Immediately!

The kind of revenue-growth strategies to transform you and your company into a profit powerhouse. Fast!

Since 1982, these principles have been tested before tough, challenging, and cynical audiences. My clients! Thousands of them. In lots of industries: Banking. Manufacturing. Wholesaling and distribution. Insurance. High tech. Media. Telecommunications. Real estate. Hospitality. Agriculture. Publishing. Building and construction. Financial services. And more.

My clients continually prove this stuff works!

Explosive production and profitability.

In August, 2001, I began working with Jodi Cornish and her team at Principal Residential Mortgage. They're fast learners! From September through December 2001, their volume exceeded the entire previous year! And 2002 was another record year. Jodi was ecstatic!

The following is from an e-mail she sent me on November 20, 2002:

"Things are moving at a frantic pace for us and we are seeing production and profitability volumes we've never seen before. And we owe that growth, in part, to you. Given all this growth, we have several new employees that I would like to request "Jeff Blackman Kits" (cassettes, books, personality inventories, etc.). We want to make sure our new hires get the same good stuff our current staff has and will need this to augment our sales training."

Jodi Cornish, Site Manager,
Principal Residential Mortgage

Most businesspeople simply don't have the time or luxury to learn all the crucial essentials of business development:

☆ Ethics.   ☆ Change.
☆ Sales.   ☆ Prospecting/Referrals.
☆ Marketing.   ☆ Creativity.
☆ Negotiations.   ☆ Time management.
☆ Customer service.   ☆ Goal achievement.

Therefore, I'll share proven, positive, and profit-producing strategies on these key areas of business growth and others—strategies to help you outdistance your competition and reach new levels of unprecedented success.

You'll soon be able to transform your corporate culture or personal approach to business with a simple yet life-changing surgical-like procedure:

The Whine-ectomy!

Moans and groans eliminated.

Complaints and whimpers eradicated.

Bellyaches and gripes removed.

No anesthesia.

No bloodshed.

No long-term pain and suffering.

Only results!

Trepidation will be turned into triumph. And if you know any wimps or whiners, they'll soon become winners!

In this practical, entertaining, and results-oriented book, you'll continually be bombarded by ideas that will:

☆ **Create breakthrough opportunities.**
☆ **Drive increased sales.**

☆ **Produce enhanced profits.**

☆ **Generate larger commissions and bigger earnings.**

Daily, you search for that competitive edge: that little bit extra; the tip, tactic, or technique that will help you penetrate an industry, establish a relationship, or secure a new deal.

You hunger for new knowledge.

Stop Whining! Start Selling! satisfies your appetite big time! It's tasty. It's meaty. It's gourmet dining!

The primary thrust is on results. After all, the name of the game in business is results—especially *your* results! Our emphasis is on loads of how-tos with a wee bit of inspiration or a dash of self-improvement.

You'll learn how to quickly grow your business and skyrocket profitability, even in a tough economy, with the help of . . .

Nine Pillars of Profit

Profit Pillar I: The Personal, Powerful You!

Profit Pillar II: Probe & Prosper

Profit Pillar III: Winning Words & Wallet Wisdom

Profit Pillar IV: A Profit Parade

Profit Pillar V: Communicate & Conquer

Profit Pillar VI: Referrals: Your Road to Results!

Profit Pillar VII: Mind & Money

Profit Pillar VIII: Serve & Soar!

Profit Pillar IX: Fly like an Eagle!

Each Profit Pillar has a series of Profit Points. For example:

☆ **Rise to the top!**
(17 considerations for crafting your impactful and results-generating "elevator speech.")

☆ **179 lessons from the network newsies.**
(179 potential power probes you can use immediately.)

☆ **Objection overruled.**
(13 driving principles to combat and overcome the four types of objections or obstacles, including sample success scripts.)

☆ **Negotiation know-how!**
(12 profit-producing and ethical strategies to enhance your negotiating savvy.)

☆ **Driving the C-class.**
(35 insights to deal with top-level decision makers.)

☆ **Get CRE8IV!**
(9 steps to boost your brain and turn creativity into cash.)

☆ **E-savvy versus Eeeh sorry!**
(15 ways to communicate with electronic or e-excellence.)

☆ **Before you bask, you must *ask*!**
(22 proven methods to ask for and get referrals.)

☆ **No-no. Yeah-yeah.**
(21 language losers to avoid, plus 27 great things to say to a prospect, customer, or client.)

☆ **21 tips for the 21ˢᵗ century.**
(21 strategies to maximize your minute management.)

**There are at least 827 business-growth strategies,
to help you grow, prosper, and win!**

Stare with your ears!

Stop Whining! Start Selling! is written the way I talk—in a no-nonsense, yet fun and conversational tone. Having been trained as a radio and TV broadcaster, I write for your ears, not just your eyes. That'll make it fun and easy for you to grab this valuable new business-growth tool and dive in—to devour a specific Profit Pillar or to simply gobble up a few Profit Points during a brief power read!

Go ahead, let your highlighter fly across a page at warp speeds. Scribble notes in the margin. Dog-ear pages to your favorite strategies. Stick Post-it Notes on key points. Choose it. Use it!

I designed this book for winners like you—folks who seek principles with a simple power and an undeniable truth: the truth that you can upgrade, improve, or enhance how you do business not in the next millennium or lifetime, but right here; right now!

Even though we just "met," there are a few things I already know about you, such as:

☆ You want to transform the lives of your clients, customers, and prospects.

☆ You want to transform your life (professionally and personally).

☆ You're serious about money and your financial future.

☆ It's important to you to make sound and intelligent financial and business decisions.

☆ You want to add dollars to your bottom line, fast.

☆ You want to sell more, achieve more, be more, and make more—

Lots more!

If you work or sell for:

☆ A Fortune 500 company.

☆ A young growth organization.

☆ A successful closely held business.

☆ A mom-and-pop operation.

☆ A start-up.

☆ An entrepreneurial-driven company.

☆ A professional or trade association.

☆ Yourself.

**You hold in your hands, right now,
a new world of infinite possibilities!**

Why now?

There's always a demand for books that are "revenue generators." *Stop Whining! Start Selling!* is such a book. **It's the shot in the arm to guide you to spectacular success.** There's no scholarly-type rhetoric. No long-winded theories. No boring lectures. Just fast-paced, street smart, straight to the point, ethical, detailed, specific actions and strategies.

You'll make more money, starting now!

While some business books tell about disappointments and down-falls, *Stop Whining! Start Selling!* shares tales of success and opportunity.

The book's title burst into my brain during the dark of night. It jolted me from a sound sleep. At 3:20 A.M., I shot up and exclaimed to my wife, "Honey, I got it!" She knew what that meant. I'd be leaving our comfy warm covers and head straight to the computer. It was time to write!

It was time to put on paper the tips, techniques, tactics, processes, and philosophies that are helping my clients deliver incredible value, maximize results, and generate big bucks.

No tricks. No smoke. No mirrors. No magic. Simply real-world solutions.

The kinda stuff my clients call "immediately implementable." Do-it-now guidance.

You can:

Read it.

Apply it.

Watch it work.

Experience its power.

Head to the bank.

Make a deposit—a big one!

Again. And again!

Guaranteed!

Heck, I wish you were paying me on a percentage basis of your new sales, commissions, and earnings!

The book's title is a title of triumph.

The more I thought about *Stop Whining! Start Selling!*, I realized the real impetus or inspiration for the book's title came from my clients. As dedicated, smart, and sincere business leaders, they love to inspire, problem-solve, and tackle tough issues. But they wanted to knock out the excuses, complaints, and whines from their folks in the field.

These leaders were frustrated and exhausted by the relentless flow of rationalized reasons they heard from their people as to why bad stuff kept preventing good stuff from happening.

Bad stuff like:

☆ There's no budget.

☆ I can't get to the decision maker.

☆ They're going in a different direction.

☆ They're happy with their current supplier.

☆ They need to think it over.

☆ The economy stinks.

☆ There's no time to consider anything new.

☆ My leads suck.

☆ We don't advertise enough.

☆ My quota isn't realistic.

☆ I'm really close to landing this one; wait till next month.

☆ I can't get past the gatekeeper.

☆ Our credit department makes it too tough to do business with us.

☆ The territory is dead.

☆ Our service team keeps screwing up my next sale.

☆ Our technology is outdated.

☆ Our compensation plan is a joke.

☆ Nobody wants to do anything till after (the new year, the meteor shower, the Chicago Cubs win a pennant).

My clients listened politely. But they wanted to stop the chaos, craziness, and commotion. They wanted their people to "stop whining and start selling!" And to find a way to "keep winning!" They simply wanted RESULTS! And so did their people. They just weren't sure how to make that happen.

Finally they made a new discovery: "See how this guy Blackman can help us."

Then they had a new realization and revelation. "Blackman's stuff really works! Learn it. Apply it. Reap the rewards!"

Others already reaping the rewards include:

Gross Income Up 30%

Brad Wuertz, a financial associate at Thrivent Financial for Lutherans, said, "My gross income increased by 30%, and a big part of that was from asking better questions. Be a sponge and soak up all of Jeff's stuff! I did and now have increased income and personal time."

A Monstrous Goal!

In November of 2000 (for the third consecutive year), I met with a client's marketing, sales, and leadership teams, where they set a monstrous, seemingly ridiculous volume goal for 2001. They didn't achieve their goal in 12 months; they blew past it in seven months!

In 2001, we once again conducted results sessions with the client's various regions. It was another record year!

This client had begun using our growth tools and strategies in 1998. One of their vice presidents sent me the following e-mail on November 29, 2002:

"This has certainly been an amazing year. We are setting records each month and we must attribute some of our success to the skills you've shared with us."

$230 Million in 23 Months!

From April 1, 1998 to March 1, 2000, our "Referrals: Your Road to Results" learning system helped Banc One Financial Services generate new sales volume directly attributable to referrals in excess of $230 million! This portfolio was sold in mid-March 2000 to Household International. (You, too, will learn how to drive referral revenue and results in Profit Pillar VI.)

Double It!

Since the fall of 1998, I've had the pleasure of working with Bob Williams and his team at Burns Sports & Celebrities. Burns is the nation's leading sports marketeer. It specializes in placing athletes, entertainers, and celebrities with corporations, ad agencies, and not-for-profits in TV commercials, ad campaigns, speaking engagements, and personal appearances.

Burns has a 30-year track record of results. And with Bob Williams' leadership since 1993 as president, Burns' revenues have increased over 500%.

In the fall of 1998, Bob asked me an interesting question: "Jeff, do you think we can double our business with these strategies?" My response was, "That's up to you! I'll provide them, yet it's the responsibility of you and your team to execute 'em!"

By December 31, 1999, Burns' business had more than doubled! And that's why, in every year since 1999, we continue our relationship for results!

So the book's title is really about a call to action—your action.

It's an exhortation for execution—your execution.

It's a command for commitment—your commitment.

It capitalizes on the basic red light/green light phenomenon of:

☆ Stop this.

☆ Do that. Go for it. Make it happen. Now!

☆ And then WIN! And keep WINNING . . . with profit-producing, explosive sales results!

After all . . .

**A crusade is about a focused, vigorous,
and concerted effort to eliminate or promote something.**

**Together, we'll eliminate whines and
promote success—your success!**

Oh yeah . . .

I already know what you're thinking: "But, Jeff, I've got every right to complain. I'm entitled to whine. I like to whine. It's cathartic. It's cleansing. Just walk in my shoes, buddy, and you'd whine, too!"

Okay, take a deep breath. Now, fire away. Whine. Complain. Yell. Scream. Jump. Shout. Slam your fist. Pound your chest. Bang the wall. Pull out your hair.

Phew! Feel better?

Is it out of your system? Behind you? Part of your past, not your present or future? If "yes," cool! If "not yet," no problem.

It'll be evolutionary, for every page takes you to more thought-provoking, action-inducing, and money-making content. With each page turn, your "whine levels" will be reduced. They'll escape from your pores, never to return. And eventually, the FDA-approved "whine-ometer" will register only a reading of "WINNER."

You'll be able to work at living, not merely live at work.
You'll be in that rarefied space known as the
"whine-free zone"!

Hey, think I can't relate? Wrong you are! I've been there, my friend. I know what it's like to ride the roller coaster. To want to whine. To crave to complain. To prefer to pout.

For as a successful sales professional or business pro, you'll experience incredible highs. Exhilaration. Victory. Awards. Recognition. Money. Pride. Achievement.

You're at the top of your ride. Building momentum. Gaining speed. Soaring toward an infinite sky.

Yet, at times, you may feel as if you're whipping around unknown curves. Plummeting through darkness. Falling uncontrollably. Doomed for disaster. Clients and prospects won't take or return your phone calls. They suddenly have selective memories. And at worst, some lie. Inexplicably, things careen out of control. And *you* feel as if you have no control.

The sure thing, the done deal, the no-brainer heads south. Your decision maker who already gave you the thumbs-up changes his or her mind, is demoted, fired, or even dies! Impossible? Nope. They've all happened to me!

So you may ask yourself, "Why am I doing this?" Because nothing happens until somebody sells something! Somebody like you. *You* make a difference.

Selling is a great ride, with far more highs than the unfortunate but occasional lows. So hop on, and enjoy your trip! I'll meet *you* at the top.

After all, you bought this book to ascend, to grow, and to prosper, plus, to be excuse-free and whine-free. Right? You bet!

Yet you also bought it to:

☆ **Create more meaningful relationships.**

☆ **Generate more sales.**

☆ **Produce greater profits.**

☆ **Develop more satisfied customers.**

☆ **Drive explosive revenue and results.**

☆ **Make more money.**

☆ **Achieve greater happiness.**

To help you do all this and a lot more, *Stop Whining! Start Selling!* is loaded with:

☆	On-target stories	☆	Impactful quotes
☆	Illustrative examples	☆	Core values
☆	Valuable lessons	☆	Powerful philosophies
☆	Amusing anecdotes	☆	Real-world solutions
☆	Profit strategies	☆	Intriguing questions
☆	Growth tips	☆	Polite challenges
☆	Proven principles	☆	Insightful interviews
☆	Tested techniques	☆	Practical counsel

Plus, along your journey, you'll also benefit from P.I.T. Stops.

Each P.I.T. Stop has:

P   Provocative or Playful

I   Inspirational or Informational

T   Thoughts or Theories

Some will make you pause and ponder. Some will make you smile. Some will make you laugh. All will make you think.

Each P.I.T. Stop will help you refuel, reenergize, and refresh yourself.

So are you ready to put your pedal to the metal? Excellent!

Then please start your engine. Shift into high gear. And together, let's begin your race toward results!

It's time to . . .

STOP WHINING!
START SELLING!

STOP WHINING!
START SELLING!
Profit-producing strategies
for explosive sales results

9 profit pillars
100 profit points
827 growth strategies

and 1 giant winner: YOU!

Profit Pillar

I

The Personal, Powerful You!

Profit Point

1

Never forget.

Never forget . . .
people invest in who you are *and* what you can do for them. One without the other assures only short-term success.

Never forget . . .
your customers, clients, and prospects invest in your ability to deliver to them a more favorable future.

Profit Point

2

World's fastest strategic lesson.

Where are you?
Where would you like to be?
How would you like to get there?

Profit Point

3

Rise to the top!

How do you respond to the question, "So, what do you do?"

If you're a typical sales professional or businessperson, you might respond with:

"I'm an account executive."

"I sell industrial supplies."

"I'm an insurance agent."

"I'm a corporate attorney."

"I'm a loan officer."

"I sell radio airtime."

"I'm a yadda, yadda, yadda."

"I specialize in blah, blah, blah."

BORING! Who cares?!

When a woman sitting behind me on a recent airplane flight was asked the "So, what do you do?" question by her seatmate, she answered, "I'm in sales."

Heck, how lame is that? Duh, we're all "in sales"! Thanks for the insight!

The preceding responses ain't eloquent elevator elixirs—as if you're riding on a rapidly moving elevator and you have only enough time between floors to make a positive impact.

Every day of your business life, you're probably asked the "So, what do you do?" question. And believe it or not, your answer has been either attracting opportunities or driving them away.

Years ago, when I was asked, "So, what do you do?" I would proudly puff my chest and exclaim, "I'm a speaker!" In retrospect, this weak and ridiculous retort merely prompted the obvious question, "Whatta ya speak on?" Perfect! (So I thought.) This was now my opening to wax rhapsodic about me.

Uh-oh. I soon discovered that although others politely listened, this was a colossal mistake. Okay, it was just plain stupid! Because little old me took a distant second to THEM! Others weren't rude; they were just far more interested in *their* stories versus mine.

Thankfully, I soon realized that to rise to the top, to ascend, I couldn't be typical. I had to be unique!

Therefore, I experimented. I played with possibilities. And then I revised my response.

So now when I'm asked, "So, what do you do?" here's my verbatim answer:

> **"I'm a business-growth specialist,**
> **who helps CEOs, entrepreneurs,**
> **their senior leadership teams, and salespeople**
> **sleep really, really well at night."**

The evolution of the preceding was inspired by a client, Jim Alland, who once said, "Blackman, you know what you're not?" Somewhat sheepishly I replied, "No, Jim, what am I not?" He answered, "You're not just a speaker, trainer, or consultant. And that's because you've had such a significant impact on our company. What you really are is a business-growth specialist."

Whoa! That was good. That simple insight became a major keeper!

My "business-growth" response generates far more interesting dialogue, because now I hear, "So, how do you do that?"—which lets me reply with, "Well, that depends. Tell me more about *your* business . . . ," followed by other nonthreatening (yet powerful) probing questions. (More on power probes in the next Profit Pillar.)

Here are four more simple yet impactful "elevator speeches":

Tax attorney:

"I show successful business owners how to keep all their wealth, every dollar of it, in the family, without losing it to the IRS."

Financial adviser:

"I show entrepreneurs like you how to have absolute control over your wealth and business, for as long as you live."

Consultant:

"I customize tools to help executives sell more, in less time, at higher profit."

Kitchen and bath designer:

"I help homeowners turn their kitchen and bath dreams into realities, so their friends and neighbors will go 'Wow!' "

To help you create your own impactful "elevator speech," here are 17 crafting considerations:

1. **Is it short?**

   Time is precious. Folks ain't interested in long-winded info-dumps, especially about you.

2. **Is it clear, concise, and easy to understand?**

   If it ain't, you're in a heap of trouble. Simplicity works. Nuthin' fancy. The goal here is to communicate. Be fast and purposeful.

3. **Is it creative or descriptive, generating intrigue and interest?**

   Creativity requires you to be innovative. Original. Imaginative. Inspired. Inventive. These are all good things! Your listeners dig flair. They're not big fans of dull and boring.

   Being descriptive helps tell a story. People love stories. Especially ones that benefit and help them . . .

   . . . to sleep really, really well at night.

   . . . to keep all their wealth.

. . . to have absolute control.

. . . to sell more in less time at higher profit.

. . . to have their friends and neighbors exclaim, "Wow!"

Intrigue and interest . . .

    create and attract . . .

        positive attention and results.

4. Is it meaningful and memorable?

Being meaningful creates immediate purpose and relevance.

Things that are memorable are unusual, different, special, or out of the ordinary, while being forgotten fosters futility and frustration, especially for you.

5. Is it conversational and natural?

Canned scripts or speeches reek of insincerity. They sound false and phony. They breed mistrust and skepticism—not exactly the fast track to success.

6. Is it capable of creating an appropriate smile, chuckle, or laugh?

When you can get somebody to smile or laugh, you have an immediate victory. A smile creates comfort, happiness, and a positive environment. This helps you lay a strong foundation early in the relationship-building and business-growth process.

7. Is it prompting a follow-up question—not a blank stare?

Questions promote dialogue. Dialogue encourages collaboration and discovery. Discovery uncovers opportunity.

Blank stares slam on the brakes! They bring conversations to a screeching and abrupt halt. That "deer-in-the-headlights" or glassy-eyed gaze of confusion turns prospects into suspects, and suspects into escape artists who want to flee your sleep-inducing rhetoric.

8. Is it identifying who you are, what you do, and, most important, who benefits and how they benefit?

Remember, decision makers invest in how you can help them attain a more favorable future.

9. **Is it quickly positioning or allowing you to politely probe and stimulate conversation and dialogue?**

   Give others the opportunity to discuss their favorite topic, themselves! You'll be surprised to discover that when somebody is yakking about *their* business, hobbies, interests, goals, and dreams, they never interrupt themselves!

10. **Is it focused on outcomes, benefits, value, and results, not yawn-inducing facts and features?**

    Facts and features are helpful, yet they are merely what something is. Outcomes, results, benefits, and value are what decision makers really invest in.

11. **Is it logically and emotionally compelling?**

    Appeal to one's mind, heart, and tummy. Decisions are influenced and made on a variety of levels. Capture as many levels as you can.

12. **Is it capable of avoiding the "Who cares?" test?**

    Ask yourself if your elevator speech passes the "Who cares?" test. Be brutally honest. If you can't give it a thumbs-up, why should somebody else?

13. **Is it working on elevators, on escalators, over the phone, at networking events, at baseball and soccer games, and at the grocery store?**

    There's only one way to find out. Try it. If it's working, cool. If it's not, tweak it. Upgrade it. And if necessary, toss it—and start over!

14. **Is it free of empty, boastful, and meaningless claims (i.e., "best, unique, superior, high-quality, state-of-the-art," etc.)?**

    When others hear hype, hyperbole, or superlatives, they immediately wonder, "Says who?" Grandiose or foolhardy claims cause listeners to retreat and seek protection beneath their b.s. deflector shields.

15. **Is it adaptable or flexible for different markets or decision makers?**

    For example, a tax attorney might say:

    "I show successful . . .

    business owners *or*

doctors *or*

corporate executives *or*

high-net-worth individuals *or*

distributors . . .

how to keep all their wealth, every dollar of it, in the family, without losing it to the IRS."

Consider how you can design and structure your "elevator eloquence" to reflect subtle changes that show expertise for a defined market or type of individual.

16. Is it easily repeated or referenced by clients and peers?

When my clients and peers began to tell others, "Jeff is a business-growth specialist," I knew my elevator speech was working. It was memorable and easily repeatable. Sweet!

17. Is it generating results?

Is there any other metric to use? Results can include:

☆ New network contacts.

☆ New prospects.

☆ New prospect meetings.

☆ New proposals or action plans.

☆ New dollars in the pipeline.

☆ New sales.

☆ New clients.

☆ New referrals.

☆ New feelings of confidence.

☆ New volume.

☆ New earnings.

Before and After

During a recent workshop, I asked each participant to turn to a partner and ask and answer the "So, what do you do?" question. Then I shared with them my "business-growth specialist" reply, plus the four others given earlier (i.e., tax attorney, financial adviser, consultant, and kitchen and bath designer).

Then I gave them the 17 crafting considerations and one more assignment. This time, they had only 90 seconds to craft a new elevator speech in response to "So, what do you do?".

The transformations were startling. For example:

1. Before: "I assist people in reaching their real estate goals."

   After: **"I counsel families and businesses on maximizing the profit potential of their current and future real estate opportunities and goals."**

2. Before: "I'm a systems engineer."

   After: **"I help you communicate with the world, quickly, efficiently, profitably."**

3. Before: "I'm a sales manager."

   After: **"I help publishers get their books into the hands of people who need them."**

4. Before: "I'm in the ticket sales department for the Minnesota Wild hockey club."

   After: **"I help businesses reach and exceed their financial goals, by helping them acquire and maintain key relationships with clients and employees."**

5. Before: "I'm in ticket sales."

   After: **"I show families the true meaning of quality time."**

6. Before: "I'm a mother."

   After: **"I shape lives for a better tomorrow."**

7. Before: "I'm a loan officer."

   After: **"I elevate people's financial stature and fulfill their financial dreams."**

Good stuff! Now, could the preceding be improved, enhanced, or upgraded? Perhaps. But remember, by design, I gave these folks only 90 seconds.

Imagine your possibilities, with the luxury of time and the bonus of thoughtful and creative deliberation.

To craft your elevator speech, jot down the key benefits, outcomes, results, and value you deliver to customers or clients.

Consider:

How do you help others maximize gain? Minimize loss?

Improve performance? Productivity? Profitability?

Grab testimonial letters or e-mails clients have sent you with words of praise. Often, the great language or insight you seek is right there in print. Adapt it. Play with it. Make it work.

Enjoy your trip, as you ride your elevator of success to the top!

Profit Point

4

You can't fly with two feet on the ground!

My United Air Lines flight lands in Boston at 3:26 P.M. Not good news, especially when my connection to Hyannis is in only 16 minutes!

I bolt off the plane at 3:32 P.M. in Logan's C terminal, spot a United customer service rep, and ask, "Where's Cape Air?"

He says, "Oh, that's easy. Walk to the end of C. Leave the building. Head to the curb. Wait for the bus that'll take you to the A terminal."

I exclaim, "Wait for the bus?"

He asks, "What time is your flight?"

My response: "3:42. Why?"

He confidently proclaims, "It'll take you about 15 minutes to get there. You'll never make it!"

I run for the curbside. Luckily, an airport shuttle bus pulls up. I hop on, grab my cell phone, call Cape Air, explain my predicament, and request they hold the plane.

The Cape Air agent says, "You're kidding." I reply, "No, I'm serious. I really need your help. Please call the gate and ask them to wait." He says, "Hang on. I'll be right back."

A minute later, he tells me, "Okay, if you can get there within the next five minutes, they'll wait."

I thank him. At 3:45 P.M., I jump off the bus, run into terminal A, and streak for the escalator. At the top, I quickly scan the gates and spot Cape Air's counter. As I'm running toward the counter, the Cape Air agent yells, "Mr. Blackman, we've been expecting you!"

I gratefully respond, "Thanks so much for your help, Lynn. How do I get to the plane?" He says, "Sorry, sir, it left."

Surprised, I exclaim, "But I thought you were expecting me?!"

"Well, we were, but we had to leave. That's our policy."

I ask, "When you say 'leave,' do you mean leave the gate or leave the ground?"

"Oh, the plane is still here, but it pulled away from the gate. So we can't board you now."

I politely say, "Lynn, I really need your help. How can you get me on that plane?"

He sternly replies, "I can't. There's nothing I can do."

I turn to Cindy, his counter compatriot. "Cindy, you look like the right person for this opportunity. Who can you talk to who will give us a 'yes' decision?"

Lynn says, "What do you mean?"

I explain to him, "I need Cindy to find somebody to say 'yes' to me. And I'm confident she will."

Lynn folds his arms and sighs, "Hmmph!"

Cindy views my request as a challenge. For I have now empowered her to rise to the occasion. To seize the moment. To grab for glory. To get me out of Boston!

Cindy grabs the phone and shouts, "*Alan*—!"

I ask, "Who's Alan?"

Lynn says, "The pilot!"

Cindy continues, "Alan! Mr. Blackman is *here*! Will you wait for him?" She then looks at me and asks, "Mr. Blackman, what do you weigh?"

I answer, "How much do you want me to weigh?"

She says, "Oh, forget it. Alan will wait for you. Run! Run!"

I fly down the stairs, shove open the tarmac door, and run to board a twin prop with Alan and four passengers.

Phew! I made it. But for the next 30 minutes, I served drinks and peanuts!

Bonus Points or Winning Ways

1. **Be politely persistent.** (Don't let bureaucracy win.)
2. **Stay calm.** (Yelling and screaming to get what you want won't work.)
3. **Be in control.** (If you're not, somebody else will be in control.)
4. **Never feel like a victim.** ("Why me?" whining doesn't serve you well. Make this a time for hope, not helplessness.)
5. **Ask questions that get you closer to your goal.** (Politely probe. Together determine what positive steps can be taken.)
6. **Spend no time with non–decision makers.** (It's a waste of time, especially if you expect them to make a decision.)
7. **Find people who can say "yes"** or can significantly influence another decision maker to say "yes." (Seek influential champions who can empathize with you, support you, or promote your cause.)
8. **Create a team.** (It's amazing what two or more dedicated people can accomplish. Let others know that you need their help.)
9. **Help another person achieve.** (Folks love to win. Let them be a positive contributor to your combined victory.)
10. **When you get the decision you want, get outta there. Fast!** (Be grateful. Say "thank you." Smile. Then split!)

Profit Point

5

Push your paradigm!

Ask yourself, your team, your leaders, your customers, your clients, and your prospects:

**"What today is impossible to do,
yet if it could be done,
would significantly change and upgrade
how you do business?"**

This is one of my favorite questions to ask clients. Why? Because it has no boundaries. No rules.

The goal is to seek and find "Cool!"

Here are two examples of when I posed this "paradigm push" question to clients.

My client:

the *World Book* Direct Marketing senior leadership team

The response:

"Hey, Jeff, wouldn't it be cool if . . .

"We could develop 3-D holographic technology, so when a child like Johnny or Susie sits in the comfort and privacy of their bedroom, playroom, or kitchen, they could touch a television screen or monitor, and hopping out of the screen would be the great male and female thinkers and leaders of all time, like Mahatma Gandhi, Susan B. Anthony, Abraham Lincoln, Florence Nightingale, Socrates, or Golda Meir. These folks could sit next to that child and then . . .

"Through artificial intelligence, that child could engage in conversations with them. Imagine a kid turning to Sir Isaac Newton and asking, 'Hey Newt, what's this physics thing, babe?' "

Cool!

My client:

Brenwick Development

(Brenwick is a real estate developer, specializing in quality and upscale homes. I was speaking to their leadership team, as well as Brenwick's customers, who are home builders.)

The response:

"Jeff, since our end-user customers are future homeowners, who find it tough to relate to a piece of property, lots of dirt, and a big hole in the ground as being their new home . .

"Wouldn't it be cool if . . .

"We could develop virtual reality helmets we pop onto the heads of prospective homeowners. Then they could take a virtual reality tour of their new home, complete with exterior landscaping, mature trees, plush thick carpeting, beautiful ceramic tile or wooden floors, a kitchen with granite countertops and top-of-the-line appliances, artistic interior lighting, and a master bedroom suite."

Cool!

Use the preceding "paradigm push" question to creatively challenge you, your team, and your leaders.

And to creatively challenge your customers, ask:

What today is impossible to do . . .
yet if it could be done . . .
would significantly change and upgrade . . .

. . . how you do business?
. . . how you grow your business?
. . . how you live your life?
. . . how you enhance your lifestyle?

Ask these or similar questions. Then listen. Intently. The answers will help you create your future—a future filled with innovative products and services, unlimited possibilities, and explosive sales. Cool!

Profit Point

6

Prospecting for gold.

Here's a surefire way to success. Always focus first on altruism, not capitalism. Commit to how you can serve others versus benefit only yourself.

To help you do just that, regularly ask others (your service providers, suppliers, vendors, attorney, accountant, banker, insurance salesperson, financial adviser, etc.) this question:

"How will I know if somebody I'm speaking with would be a good prospect, customer, or client for you?"

Or make the following statement:

"Tell me more about your ideal customer or client, so when I'm out and about in the community, I can keep my eyes and ears open for you."

How's that for an easy, yet powerful question or success statement? Whenever I use the preceding, I hear comments like:

"Thanks, Jeff, that was very thoughtful of you to ask!"
"I really appreciate your interest!"
"Whoa, nobody has ever asked me that!"

Remember: To achieve the extraordinary, don't be ordinary. Because for profits to peak, you must be unique!

Profit Point

7

Passion produces profit.

Passion is mandatory! There must be a fire in your belly, a passion in your gut, a sense of excitement in your sinew. You must have a missionary zeal along with a relentless pursuit to satisfy your customers, clients, and prospects.

Your passion has nothing to do with phony smiles, clever phrases, and banners with slogans. It means your ability and desire to compete profitably now and throughout the 21st century.

Passion is burning the midnight oil. It's going the extra mile. It's doing the unexpected. Passion is your positive attitude in a world of negativity. It's finding the extra fuel when you thought your tank was dry. It's an unwillingness to accept second best or to say, "It's good enough."

Passion somehow lets you execute, even when you're exhausted. Passion confidently pits you against your toughest competitor—you.

Passion converts suspects into prospects. Prospects into customers. And customers into friends for a lifetime.

Passion turns successful salespeople into superstars!

Profit Point

8

A great eight!

While I always stress the importance of asking others great questions (see the next Profit Pillar), here are a "great eight" to politely challenge and inspire you:

1. Let's imagine we walk out together into your future for _____ years. When you look back at that time, what would you have liked to accomplish? (With you? Your family? Your career? Your business?)

2. If anything in your world or future could come true, what would that include?

3. What would you most like to change in your life? How willing are you to make these changes? When will you make them?

4. What's your biggest piece of unfinished business in your professional life? How about personal life? What steps will you take to "finish" them?

5. What brings you the greatest happiness? How are you going to make sure you have more of that happiness in your life?

6. What kinds of resources could be redirected to achieve your goals?

7. What activities, experiences, events, or moments would make your life complete? What steps will you take to make these things happen?

8. And perhaps the most challenging question: What's the risk of doing nothing?

Profit Point

9

A fish story!

I have a love/hate relationship with fishing!

What I hate about it is that it's slow. It ruins a good boat ride. And it becomes a very expensive nap!

What I love about it is that it teaches you important lessons, personally and professionally.

What I especially love about it is that it provides quality time with those who are important to me: My son. My dad. My brother-in-law. My nephews. My friends. And their kids.

We have landed little nibbles and big ones in lakes, rivers, gulf waters, and oceans.

Some of the valuable lessons learned while fishing are:

1. **Persistence pays.** (Refuse to quit.)

2. **Always seek new pools of possibilities.** (Sounds like prospecting.)

3. **Dangle the hook and bait in the water in front of the fish.** (Sounds like marketing.)

4. **When the fish bites, set the hook and reel him in.** (Sounds like selling.)

5. **Bait your hook with what the fish likes to eat.** (Sounds like negotiating.)

6. **Once the fish is caught, keep him comfortable.** (Sounds like customer service.)

7. **Attitude matters, yet you're compensated for your behavior and results.**

8. **Listen to the experts**—for example, Captain Jimbo Hail, who taught me how to jig in the Gulf of Mexico.

9. **Don't brood over rejection.** It's more fun to talk about the one you reeled in than the one that got away.

10. **You've gotta be in the right place at the right time.** And then know what to do while you're there!

11. **Reap the rewards**—for example, having red snapper we hooked in the gulf, prepared by a gourmet chef at a local hotel's restaurant within two hours from the time we caught it.

So how can you always find a great fishing hole with plenty of fish?

Here's a simple yet profit-peaking exercise.

Answer these 10 questions as they apply to you, your products or services, your business, your prospects, your customers or clients, and your marketplace.

1. What are your customers' critical success considerations (CSCs)? (What are the factors that matter most to them and influence whether they're willing to give you and your company approval?)

2. What have been your most successful strategies to build your business?

3. What buying trends are you seeing?

4. What other organizations or businesses serve your prospects or target markets, with whom you might create a strategic alliance?

5. What professional organizations do your prospects belong to? (How can you create and attain visibility within these groups?)

6. What trade, consumer, or professional publications do your prospects read? How can you position yourself as an expert (i.e., as a contributing writer, a resource for interviews, etc.)?

7. Do you have unique benefits or hidden assets about your company and people that your prospects could receive significant value from, yet you're not telling them? (If so, what are these benefits or assets?)

8. What specific problems are you solving in a prospect's or customer's life?

9. What results and outcomes do you deliver to customers?

10. What are the top 10 reasons a decision maker should buy from you and your company, rather than from a competitor?

Bonus Points or Winning Ways

1. Daily, conduct the world's fastest strategic plan by answering:

    > Where are you?
    > Where would you like to be?
    > How would you like to get there?

2. To gain market share, capture mind share. Create favorable impressions about how you can positively impact others.

3. Find out what everybody else is doing, then don't do it! It's okay to emulate, just don't imitate. Instead, innovate!

4. Realize that you're rewarded for behavior and performance, not intent.

5. Know your metrics. What's working? What ain't? Measure results (i.e., new customers, average sale increases, deeper penetration and growth with current customers, dollars in the pipeline, sales volume, etc.).

Profit Point

10

A champion's vision.

In the spring of 2000, I consulted with Bill Russell. Russell is one of the most celebrated athletes in the history of sports. His feats of victory read more like a "believe it or not" tale than a resume of remarkable results.

His accomplishments include:

☆ Eleven National Basketball Association (NBA) world championships in 13 seasons with the Boston Celtics.

☆ NBA Hall of Famer.

☆ Only athlete to ever win two NBA championships as a player/coach.

☆ Voted one of the top 50 NBA players of all time.

☆ Two NCAA championships with the University of San Francisco.

☆ Olympic gold medal winner.

☆ Recognized by HBO as the greatest winner of the 20th century.

One of the most interesting stories Russell told me was about his role as a rebounder.

Russell did more than merely elevate his angular 6′10″ body to grab the ball or "wipe the glass" following an opponent's errant shot. Instead, he turned rebounding into a science.

Russell studied other players. He learned their tendencies—their shot patterns, their habits, especially the bad ones. This analysis gave him a competitive advantage.

When an opponent launched a shot, other players followed the ball. Not Russell. Instead, he fought for position in more valuable territory. He was headed to where the ball was going, after it hit the backboard or rim on a missed shot.

This strategy, dogged determination, and exhaustive preparation helped Russell become the most prolific rebounder of his time. (He averaged 22.5 per game and led the league in rebounding four times.)

But Russell knew once he had the ball, he had to get rid of it. Fast! His next goal was to quickly fling the ball downcourt via an outlet pass to a streaking teammate. With speed and precision, Russell would grab a rebound and hurl a pass up the hardwood.

He wasn't throwing to a teammate as much as he was throwing to a spot—a spot a teammate would suddenly fill so he could dribble to the bucket or pass to another teammate. The result: two more fast-break Celtic points.

Throughout a game, Russell would toss a lot of so-called no-look or blind passes. He told me the "blind" pass is a misnomer because "Tossing the ball to a player you can't see is dumb!" And Russell ain't dumb.

When I asked how he perfected the outlet pass, he rose before me, extended his long arms in front of his body, spread the fingers of his enormous hands, and said, "I worked on and improved my peripheral vision. Every day, I'd slowly extend each hand. A little to the left. A little to the right."

Eventually, his hands, though his arms were extended from his sides like a bird's awesome wingspan, were still in his line of sight. Just like on the court where a streaking open teammate would take Russell's bullet pass in full stride and head for the hoop.

Russell said, "Clear peripheral vision gives you focus. You have to rid yourself of peripheral opponents."

Lessons

☆ Keep your eyes open for opportunity.

☆ Remember that results require teamwork and time.

☆ Prepare for victory.

☆ Work smart, every day.

☆ Focus.

☆ Develop your strengths.

☆ See what others don't see, then take action.

"You have to believe you are great. You have to have an air about you. Every time I step on that field, I want to prove I am the best player in the league. I want it more than anybody."

—Brett Favre, quarterback, Green Bay Packers, and three-time National Football League Most Valuable Player

P.I.T. Stop

P Provocative or Playful

I Inspirational or Informational

T Thoughts or Theories

Here Comes the Bride?

My wife met a woman who had recently announced her engagement, but she stressed her wedding wouldn't happen for at least two years. When my wife asked why, she exclaimed, "I want to wait, just in case something better comes along."

I'll Make It Up on Volume

Bruce Bunescu, an account representative with Boise Cascade Office Products, told me:

> "A customer wanted to buy an item at a lower price than we normally charged. When I told her that price was $5 below my cost and I couldn't sell it for a loss, she said, 'But I want to buy three of them!'"

Height of Absurdity

From my "adults say the funniest and darnedest things" collection:

> *"Jeff, nice to finally meet you. I've been reading your magazine columns for years. You're much taller than your picture!"*
>
> *—A workshop participant*

> *"Things turn out best . . . for those who make the best . . . out of the way things turn out."*
>
> *—John Wooden, legendary UCLA basketball coach*

Profit Pillar

II

Probe & Prosper

Profit Point

11

Conquer with questions.

Chocolate or vanilla?

Aisle or window?

Will you marry me?

Work or play?

Would you like to super size to large fries?

Questions! Every day, we ask and answer hundreds of 'em personally and professionally. And after doing so (especially asking them), you'd think one would be pretty good at it. Well, here's the bad news: Most salespeople are pitiful probers.

When I ask salespeople to share with me a "dynamic dozen" of their top 12 open-ended need development questions, they stare at me like I'm nuts. And when I request they recite them devoid of "ums" or "ahs" and without any sense of hesitation, reluctance, or delay, they start throwing stuff at me!

Your ability to question or probe is one of your most important and profit-producing sales tools.

Yet all too often, salespeople assume their success is dependent on their ability to master their "pitch, spiel, or presentation." It's not!

While that's a part of the sales process, in the long run your investigative or questioning skill is the most direct route to help you achieve new levels of success and profitability.

The discovery, questioning, or probing process enables you to uncover:

☆ What problems your customers or prospects have to solve.

☆ What needs they'd like to fill.

☆ What dreams they'd like to realize.

This strategy gives you tremendous insight into one's likes and dislikes, sense of commitment, budget, expectations, and objectives.

Failure to properly assess these things causes most salespeople to flounder. And they wonder why. Their assumptions are:

"Gee, I must be a poor closer."

"I guess I need more product knowledge."

"I knew that customer was just browsing, anyway!"

Assumptions and excuses like these have no place in the probe, prosper, and results process.

There's room for only value-driven principles and knowledge—knowledge of your customers, clients, prospects, industry, products, and marketplace. Remember, knowledge pays handsome dividends. And the best way to obtain knowledge about others is with effective questioning.

The real success of my interviews as a radio and TV broadcaster depends not on my speaking ability, but on my ability to question. Questions give me the opportunity to explore a guest's feelings, attitudes, and opinions. Exactly like the sales interview.

Yet it requires preparation. Lots of it.

You can't wing it!

Before every meeting with a prospect or client (in person or over the phone), I prepare. How? First and foremost, with a list of key questions. Clients even kid me at the start of a meeting: "Jeff, how many questions have you got for today's discussion?"

Questions allow you to discover whether a customer or prospect has a motivated or unmotivated need. Somebody with a motivated need has a problem to solve. An unmotivated need, no matter how eloquent your sales presentation, is unlikely to lead to a sale. Why? Because the prospect has no pain to diminish, problem to solve, or dream to realize.

Profit Point

12

Rain, rain, go away!

Several years ago, I was conducting a three-day sales and marketing workshop in Toledo, Ohio. Immediately following the conclusion of the first day's program, I changed into my jogging clothes and hit the pavement. At the half-mile point it began to pour. Despite this unwelcome and unexpected drenching, I continued to run, eventually seeking protection in a nearby shopping mall.

Upon entering the mall, I was quickly greeted by a cheery representative of a major retail chain department store. She immediately inquired, "Sir, how'd you like to fill out an application for our charge card?" I assured her I didn't need more "plastic money"! She then acknowledged my tired, cold, and damp condition and asked, "Just for applying, you receive at no obligation . . ." She then reached beneath the counter and brought out an umbrella! "You'd find this umbrella helpful, wouldn't you?" I said, "Where do I sign?!" I had a motivated need!

Motivated needs are easily discovered through observation, a natural curiosity, and especially the question-and-answer process.

As a sales pro . . .

> **You should never sell, tell, reveal, or demonstrate your product or service until your prospect or customer's specific needs have been discovered and are understood.**

Like a physician, you can't suggest, recommend, or advocate until you know what you need to remedy. Think back to your last doctor's visit. Did you enter the office, linger in the reception area, wait in a cold examining room, and then eventually have your doctor arrive and proclaim, "Looks like you're here for stress. Ummm, how about the flu? No, no, let me guess—a pulled muscle, would you believe. . . "?

It's unlikely you'd have confidence in *this* doc's diagnosis! He guessed at your ailments. He didn't allow you to share the symptoms of your illness. But what do competent doctors do? They ask lots of questions, like, "What hurts? How long have you been suffering? Has this ever happened before?"

Once these questions are answered, then and only then can a proper treatment be offered or a medication prescribed. How can you "prescribe" unless you, too, first "examine"? Remember, prescription without diagnosis is malpractice!

The benefits of asking questions are numerous. Here are seven distinct advantages:

1. Your customers, clients, and prospects share their **feelings from their perspective.**

2. You **gain valuable insights** into your prospects and customers as individuals.

3. You begin to **appreciate their needs.**

4. If you say something, it's likely to be true. **If your prospects, customers, and clients say something, it's gospel!**

5. When your customers and prospects speak, they may **reveal a need or problem you had not previously considered.**

6. The sales presentation's **focus is on your prospect** or customer's presentation of information versus the traditional salesperson's "spiel, pitch, or dog and pony show."

7. **Questions put you in control.** Though your prospects, clients, and customers seemingly dominate the sales process, interview, or discovery stage with their ideas, that's fine. Let them! They think they're in control. Yet with questions, *you* are!

Profit Point

13

Good-bye to gab.

"What a smooth talker!" "She's got the gift of gab!" Or, "He's a born salesman!" How many times have you heard remarks like these? Lots? You bet. But to the best of my knowledge, salespeople are never born! My obstetrician friends assure me they have never hoisted a newborn and proudly announced to the parents, "Congratulations! You've given birth to a salesperson!"

Successful salespeople don't inherit their skills.
They are nurtured, developed, and educated.
At least the top achievers are!

They may have the ability to gab or talk, but their real talent is their skill to probe or question. Questions establish rapport, uncover concerns, and reveal problems. Questions are a natural way to get others to talk, so *you* can *listen* and *learn*. This assures that you never sell from ignorance!

Profit Point

14

The answer is in the question!

Power probing, interviewing, or discovery techniques will have a dramatic impact on your bottom line and earnings. You shouldn't begin to suggest or solve before you've asked or analyzed.

When I meet prospective clients for the first time, they often ask me, "How can you help us?" My response is, "I don't know. At this point, I'm really not sure. Because it's likely your needs are different and unique, in comparison to others I've helped. Therefore, would it be okay to ask you just a few questions to better understand your unique needs and specific concerns?" No one has ever said "No!"

To maximize your results during your probing or discovery process, here are six profit-producing tips:

1. Let your prospects and customers know **you need to ask questions** so you can better help them.

2. **Always ask for their permission** or okay before you start the probing process.

3. When your prospects, clients, and customers are talking, **don't interrupt.**

4. **Take lots of notes.** There's great credibility in the written word, especially when the words belong to your prospect or customer. Words not written down are words forgotten. (A law school professor of mine used to say, "An oral contract is as good as the paper it's written on!") Also, be sure to ask for permission to take notes. The reason you ask for their approval or okay is you want them to be comfortable, trusting, and willing to share information. If you suddenly pull out a legal pad and start scribbling away, others could become reluctant and unwilling participants. Usually I'll say something like, "I don't want to miss a word of what you're saying—this is really good stuff. Would you mind if I jot down some notes?" Nobody has ever refused. And people have literally handed me their pens and legal pads.

5. **Converse, don't interrogate.** There's no need to play Sergeant Joe Friday of *Dragnet* fame: "The facts, ma'am, just the facts." Instead, follow the example of actor Peter Falk's famous TV character, Detective Lieutenant Columbo. His questions were asked almost apologetically. They seemed harmless. However, they uncovered information that always led to a solved case. Your "case" can best be solved by in essence never presenting your case. Rather, let your decision makers present their case by responding to your skillfully asked questions.

6. **Jot down your key need-development questions**, so they become automatic. Put them on a three-by-five-inch card or even record them onto a cassette. Burn a CD. Keep them close to your phone. In your briefcase. Taped to your car's visor. In your car's audio/CD player. Wherever they'll serve as a constant reminder that **questions seldom fail to secure a sale.**

Profit Point

15

Mr. Big said, "Sell me!"

Some time ago, I had a meeting with the head partner (we'll call him Mr. Big) of a large and well-recognized financial organization. The purpose of our meeting was to discuss a series of seminars in an ongoing learning system for his professional staff. We had never met, and he was the final decision maker. My proposal or action plan had already been approved by the firm's marketing director, assistant director of human resources, and director of human resources. They all told me they were confident that it would get Mr. Big's okay as well.

When I entered Mr. Big's office (about the size of Texas), the marketing director and assistant director of human resources rose to greet me and introduce me to Mr. Big. I extended my hand to Mr. Big, and as we shook hands, he stared straight at me and without acknowledging my greeting tersely stated, "Sell me!" Was this a request? No way. It was a challenge!

Although I was tempted to *tell* him how productive and profitable I'd make his team, I didn't. I knew that would be a crucial mistake, violating my own principles of being an effective power prober. Instead, I looked directly back at him and said, "To help you maximize results, do you mind if I ask you a few questions?" He said, "No, fire away!" I then asked:

"What do you like about the action plan?"

"How does it help you achieve your objectives?"

"What would you add or delete from the learning system?"

"What do you want your people to leave with?"

"How soon do you want your people to benefit from these new skills . . . to produce enhanced results?" (This is obviously a much better question than simply asking, "When should we schedule the first program?").

As he responded to these and other questions, I wrote like a madman. The entire meeting lasted 50 minutes. Of those 50 minutes, I spoke for maybe 8 to 10 minutes. The rest of the time, I asked questions and simply listened. At the 50th minute, Mr. Big gazed over his glasses and delivered his royal decree: "All right, Blackman, I'm confident. I'm convinced. Let's do it!"

I thanked him for his time, cooperation, and most importantly *his* valuable input. I didn't talk him into buying. I listened him into investing. Despite his request or challenge of "Sell me!" I didn't "sell him." He sold himself!

Werner Heisenberg, a Nobel prize-winning physicist once stated, "Nature does not reveal its secrets; it only responds to our method of questioning." Therefore, let "nature" take its course. Use questions! Questions reveal needs. Needs lead to solutions. Solutions create sales. Let me repeat that:

Questions reveal needs.
Needs lead to solutions.
And solutions create sales.

. . . sales that help you and others attain a more favorable future. And that's important to you . . . isn't it?

Profit Point

16

When is it over?

I often ask clients and workshop participants, "How do you know when you've finished the probe or discover stage?" Their typical responses are:

"When you've run out of questions."

"When the customer wants to see what you've got."

"When you think you know all there is to know."

"When they start asking you questions."

All of these answers are logical, but not correct. Why? Because it ain't over till the customer says it's over!

Before I ever begin to reveal or show a client how I can help, I inquire (at what I think is the likely end of the probe or discover stage), "What other information would you like to share with me before I suggest some results strategies and creative solutions in an action plan?" If the response is, "Can't think of anything else; you've got it all," then and only then do I move on to the next step: scheduling the meeting to present an action plan and seek commitment. If they want to share even more information, I respectfully and intently listen.

Profit Point

17

Child's play.

When you're a parent, there are lots of important people in the lives of your children: Mom, Dad, siblings, grandparents, friends, family, teachers, coaches, doctors, and, of course, babysitters!

Babysitters are valuable human capital, because the good ones are really tough to find. When our kids were younger, my wife would be on a relentless mission to discover the perfect one. Somebody who was reliable. Resourceful. Punctual. Organized. Neat. Friendly. Respectful.

Heck, those assets are hard to find in an adult! Now imagine trying to find them in a neighborhood 12-year-old who has not yet fallen prey to dating, shopping malls, and hanging out with a horde of friends. It ain't easy!

Until . . .

One day, years ago, my wife enthusiastically screeched from the kitchen, "Jeffery, I finally found her!" I replied, "Found who?" She said, "A great babysitter, Jaclyn." She was right. Jaclyn was a quality find. Our kids would love her.

And then Sheryl said something I didn't expect: "Jeffery, please go to the fax machine." Somewhat surprised, I asked, "For what?" She answered, "Oh, to help Jaclyn prepare for next Saturday night. She wants to fax us some questions."

Although dazed and confused, I slogged toward the fax machine. There, waiting for me, was a two-page fax from a 12-year-old!

Blackmans' Info.

Fire:

Police:

Poison control:

Doctor (name and phone number):

Where parents can be reached (phone number):

Full address where I am babysitting:

Town:

Phone:

Neighbor (name, address, and phone number):

Other instructions:

page 1

Where will you be?

Are there any rooms off-limits?

What time should the kids go to sleep?

Do the kids have any health problems?

Should we expect visitors?

What should kids eat?

(I suggested the visitors!)

Can we go outside? How long can we be out? Where can we go?

Will you be calling? When?

Should I do anything for your animals?

(I suggested complete grooming!)

Kids—names and ages:

Do you have any hunting weapons?

If yes, are they locked up?

page 2

Jaclyn was taught to ask impactful and meaningful questions during a six-hour babysitting certification program taught by our community's fire department. Pretty impressive stuff!

Would you hire Jaclyn? If so, you'll now have to negotiate with her agent and business manager!

Since Jaclyn can ask great questions, so can you!

Profit Point

18

179 lessons from the network newsies.

Great journalists ask great questions. Questions that seek the truth. Uncover new information. Elicit opinions and emotions. You should do the same.

Just like a great journalist, your probing questions should start with:

☆	Who?	☆	Why?
☆	What?	☆	Which?
☆	When?	☆	How?
☆	Where?	☆	Tell me more about . . .

These open-ended questions can be mixed (where appropriate) with closed-ended questions requiring a "yes" or "no" response to maximize your questioning savvy.

Closed-ended questions aren't bad. Sometimes they're essential, especially for qualification purposes. However, a closed-ended question doesn't promote dialogue; it brings it to a screeching halt. It doesn't help you understand the emotion, motivation, or gut-level feeling of a reply.

Questions help one: think, imagine, envision, wonder, consider, explore, dare, pursue, dream, believe, ponder, play, capture, and seize the possibilities.

The following questions are designed to get your prospects, clients, and customers to *open up*. Are they all-inclusive? Of course not. Can you use and apply all of them? Perhaps—although not necessarily in the same call, visit, or meeting. But do they help you fine-tune your questioning and earning power? Definitely, yes! The results are remarkable. Heck, they're explosive and profit-producing!

Some questions are similar. The only nuance might be a word's inclusion, exclusion, or placement. While the distinction might be subtle, the impact could be profound. Adapt and work with the words, phraseology, and questions that best complement you, your personality, your customers, your level of decision makers, your products, your services, or your sales situation.

And then:

Practice.

Prepare.

Rehearse.

Prep some more.

Execute.

"The facts are always friendly; every bit of evidence one can acquire, in any area, leads one that much closer to what is true."

—*Carl Rogers*

Here are 179 potential power probes:

1. (Name), to help you like I've/we've helped other extremely satisfied customers/clients achieve their goals, I/we need to ask you some quick questions. First, let's focus on your business (goals, issues, concerns, challenges, etc.).

2. What are your goals—short-term/long-term? What are you looking to accomplish?

3. What challenges are you facing in growing your business?

4. What are your priorities?

5. What are your strategic initiatives for (Q1, Q2, the year)?

6. So I don't forget what matters most to you, do you mind if I take notes? (A closed-ended question, but nobody will object.)

7. What are you doing to improve or upgrade your current . . . ?

8. How would you like to improve your current . . . ?

9. What is it about this strategy that looks appealing, that sounds on-target?

10. What does your perfect solution look like?

11. How valuable would it be if I could share with you strategies our team has used to help others like you pursue and achieve their goal(s) of . . . ?

12. What have been some of your concerns when previously considering . . . ? What can I do to make sure those concerns never happen when you work with me and your (reference your company's name) team?

13. What's your biggest challenge?

14. What additional information do you think is important for me to know before I suggest some strategies, options, or solutions that will help you (solve your problem, meet your need, accomplish your goal, realize your dream)?

15. What are the qualities you look for in (a law firm, a strategic partner, etc.)?

16. How soon would you like to implement a plan and a direction that will help you . . . ? (Refer to their specific goals, issues, etc.)

17. What will you value most in our relationship?

18. What matters most to you about . . . ?

19. What are your key performance or profitability indicators? How would those be jeopardized by . . . ? Or without . . . ?

20. What's the best business decision you ever made?

*"Curiosity is one of the most certain and perma-
nent characteristics of a vigorous intellect."*
—*Samuel Johnson*

21. What in your business brings you the greatest happiness?

22. Let's imagine we walk out together into the future for _____ years. When you look back at that time, what would you like to have accomplished?

23. How might time become your enemy if you choose to do nothing?

24. How can I help you, then, achieve your goal(s) or solve your problem(s)?

25. Why do you think it's so important that we consider this now?

26. Where are you now? Where would you like to be? How would you like to get there?

27. Let's imagine (refer to a specific goal, problem, or issue the client states) comes true. How does that make you feel? What would the impact be?

28. What's the risk of doing nothing?

29. If anything in your world could come true, what would that be?

30. Over the next _____ months/years, what would you like to be your biggest triumphs?

31. What would you most like to change about your current situation?

32. What kind of resources could be redirected to achieve your goals?

33. Do I have your okay or permission to be politely persistent until the job gets done, realizing that where we go from here is strictly and totally up to you? (Another closed-ended question, but a really good one because it confirms their commitment. Plus, gives you permission to follow up.)

34. What's the biggest headache about your current situation that you'd like to eliminate?

35. What keeps you up at night?

36. What questions do you have that will help me help you?

37. When can you come in? (Suggest week, date, time, etc.)

38. I'm more than happy to come to your office; however, if interruptions are likely, it may take even more time and that's not fair to you. So when can you come in? (Suggest week, date, time, etc.)

39. Within the next two to three weeks, what are the best opportunities for us to get together? (Suggest week, date, time, etc.)

40. Since your needs and goals may change, when would you like me to call you back? (Suggest time frame.)

"See it like it is!"
—Herb Cohen

41. In the unlikely event I don't hear from you, when would you like me to call you back? Or when should I call you again?

42. That's interesting. Why do you feel that way? What makes you say that?

43. Tell me more about your . . .

44. How valuable would it be to share with you strategies our team has used to help others like you to . . . ? (Be specific.)

45. What is most important to you about . . . ?

46. What have been some of your frustrations when previously working with or going through (a financial adviser, a distributor, a loan process, etc.)? What can I do to make sure that never happens when you work with me and your team at (reference your company)?

47. If you won the lottery today, what would you do?

48. If time and money weren't concerns, what would you do?

49. What are your life/family/business priorities?

50. What are the qualities you look for in (an adviser, a strategic partner, an accountant, a real estate agent, etc.)?

51. Who are some of your other valued professionals or advisers? How often do you visit with them? How helpful to you would it be to get them involved early in our discussion?

52. How do you define . . . ?

53. How would you define your level of or tolerance for risk?

54. Tell me more about how you feel about risk.

55. What would happen to (you, your family, your business) if you did/didn't . . . ?

56. What trouble, if any, do you have with . . . ?

57. What challenges, if any, do you have with . . . ?

58. What matters most to you about (money, your people, your results, your image, your lifestyle, etc.)?

59. Who do you rely on for answers to tough (financial, legal, marketing, distribution, etc.) questions you can't answer? Why do you call them? How have they been able to help you?

60. Who else might you discuss this with? When would you like me/us to visit with him/her/them?

"When you 'hold' a conversation, be sure to 'let go' once in a while!"

61. What makes you happy?

62. What's the best decision you ever made?

63. Let's divide your goals into two categories, short-term and long-term. What do you want to accomplish with your short-term goals? And long-term?

64. What kind of special problems or challenges might exist that are important for me to know about? (Personal? Family? Business?)

65. When you talk about *you*, what would *you* like to do, not for your family or business, only *you*. What would *you* like to see and do?

66. What would you like for your family?

67. What would you like for your business?

68. What if you had no worries or concerns about (your family or your business)? Suppose everything regarding them was already taken care of; with that under control, what then would you like to do or accomplish?

69. What brings you the greatest happiness (hunting, fishing, golf, etc.)?

70. What are your plans for . . . ?

71. How do you intend to accomplish that?

72. How can I help?

73. Why do you think it's so important that we consider this now?

74. Let's pretend/imagine (fact scenario). How does that make you feel?

75. Let's gaze into the future _____ years. How does that make you feel?

76. When you had previously selected that product or service, what was your motivation? What were you hoping to accomplish?

77. How would that fit?

78. What's best about . . . ?

79. How will this benefit you?

80. When you say "good" . . . compared to what?

"The key to your universe is that you can choose."
—*Carl Frederick*

81. If anything in your world or your future could come true, what would you include?

82. What would your world look like if all your wishes came true?

83. To give me an even better understanding, we can start with either your current challenges and obstacles or your future goals, hopes, and dreams. What's your preference?

84. Which is more important to you—a bargain or value and results?

85. What matters most about _____ to you?

86. Is this problem growing? Stable? Declining? (Tell me more.)

87. When you addressed this before, what happened?

88. What has changed since our last visit? What else should we address?

89. What needs to change, for us to . . . ?

90. Over the next _____ years, what would you like to be your biggest triumphs?

91. Over the next _____ years, what would you like to be your major indulgences?

92. If money was no object, how would you spoil yourself? Your family? Your employees?

93. What brings you the greatest joy?

94. How are you going to make sure you have more of that joy in your life?

95. What would you most like to change about your current . . . ?

96. How willing are you to make these changes?

97. How soon would you like to make these changes?

98. What words best describe your attitude about . . . ?

99. What's your biggest piece of unfinished business personally? With your family? With your business?

100. Once your headaches about _____ are under control, what impact would that have?

> **"When you talk you can only say something that you already know. When you listen, you may learn what someone else knows."**

101. Aside from yourself, who else might be involved in:

    . . . us working together?

    . . . approving this decision?

    . . . giving the green light to help you achieve your goals?

. . . the decision-making process?

. . . giving the thumbs-up?

102. Have I explained that well?

103. Have I made that clear?

104. Have I done a good job explaining this?

105. Did I make this easy to understand?

106. How will this action plan help you achieve your goals?

107. Your feelings about _____ are . . .

108. What's your opinion about . . . ?

109. What do you think about . . . ?

110. How do you feel about . . . ?

111. Your comfort level with _____ is . . .

112. What would happen if . . . ?

113. How important is it to take care of this now so (you, your partner, employees, your spouse, children, etc.) don't have to take care of it tomorrow?

114. Which strategy would you like to use: 1, 2, or 3?

115. How would you like to protect . . . ?

116. How would you like to grow . . . ?

117. What is your greatest concern (business, financial, or otherwise)?

118. What do you like best about your current . . . ?

119. What do you like least about your current . . . ?

120. What do you want us to focus on?

"Our aspirations are our possibilities."
—Robert Browning

121. How can I be most effective in . . . ?

122. What would you like to accomplish with . . . ?

123. How have you strategically planned for . . . ?

124. How would (you, your family, your business, etc.) be affected if . . . ?

125. How do you envision . . . ?

126. How's your _____ performing?

127. What do you want your _____ to do for you?

128. What is your greatest fear about . . . ?

129. If you could design a perfect solution, what would it include?

130. What's the purpose/goal for that (money, budget, etc.)?

131. What are your goals for _____ ? How will you achieve them? How can I help you achieve them? How can we work together to help you achieve them?

132. What's the most important thing in your (life, business) right now?

133. How do you plan to handle . . . ?

134. If I could show you a way to _____ , how important would that be to you?

135. Other satisfied clients/customers in situations similar to yours have found it's most beneficial to do. . . . How do you feel about that, or how will that work for you?

136. If you could design your own _____ , what would be the top benefits? Or what would you want to make sure it could do?

137. What circumstances would have to occur or what needs to change for you to . . . ?

138. Without this (plan, solution, machine, etc.), how are you going to improve your . . . ?

139. What is it about this solution you're uncomfortable with? Unsure of? Hesitant about? Reluctant with?

140. We have other members of our team who will devote close attention to (you, your business and its success, your family and your progress—give names/roles, etc.). How would you feel about also hearing from them?

"Silence is man's chief learning."
—*Palladas*

141. How would you like me/us to keep you informed about the progress we're making: Via mail? Phone? E-mail? A combination?

142. What's the risk of taking no action?

143. What's the risk of delaying your decision?

144. What interests you most about this?

145. How would you like to pursue this?

146. What can we do to make this work?

147. What's the purpose/reason/motivation for your . . . ?

148. How soon would you like to . . . ?

149. Which is of greatest interest: A, B, or C?

150. How valuable is it to you to work with a proven and reliable partner like (reference your company)? What do you value most?

151. What might you be gambling or sacrificing to work with somebody else?

152. How would you feel if you learned too late that a competitor of mine misrepresented their capabilities about products, services, or reputation?

153. What impact might that misrepresentation have on (you, your family, your business, etc.)?

154. How much time might be lost?

155. How much money might be lost?

156. How does their _____ compare to our _____?

157. What strategy would help you deliver the greatest results or produce the most desired outcomes?

158. How soon would you like to move to the next step, so that you can . . . (refer to their specific goals).

159. Why do you think it's so important we take action now?

160. Aside from me/us/(your company), who else are you considering? Working with? What do you like best about them? What do you wish they offered, but they don't? Why is that so important to you? How will that help you?

"Action conquers fear."
—*Peter Nivio Zarlenga*

161. How did you hear about us?

162. What are your expectations?

163. How will we measure success?

164. What can we do to make sure this is an easy and hassle-free experience for you and your family or your business?

165. What are your strategic initiatives?

166. What trends are impacting your business?

167. How might your needs change in the future?

168. What else is important for us to (consider, review, discuss, anticipate, plan for, think about, etc.)?

169. What criteria do you use to make a decision?

170. Please describe your decision-making process.

171. You said it would be better to call you in 30 days—that's great. Between now and then, what changes or differences will make your life easier or would you like to see happen?

172. What helps you and your company stay successful?

173. When is the best time to. . .

174. If you could create the perfect _____ (product, service, solution), what would you require?

175. What would be the ideal way for us to help you?

176. What type of disappointment or frustration have you experienced or suffered with or when using . . . ?

177. How have (you, your team, people, customers, clients) reacted to . . . ?

178. How would this (increase in sales, decrease in attrition, improvement in performance, elimination of repetitive steps, etc.) impact your business projections over the next (quarter, year, etc.)?

179. If a 24-hour restaurant never closes, why are there locks on the doors?

Obviously, the questions you could ask are endless. As a power prober and peak profiteer, be sure to create *your* list of *core* potential probing or need-development questions. You can even organize them by key categories—for example, business history, marketing and sales, competition, operations, technology, physical facilities, management, training, lifestyle, personal dreams and goals, or any logical category that makes sense for your products or services.

To best familiarize yourself with the discovery or probe questions that'll work best for you, I strongly suggest, repeatedly recommend, and unequivocally urge you to write them down! Michael Spak, one of my law school professors, once said, "Pale ink is better than a faded memory." You may even want to record your questions on cassette or CD so when you drive to appointments, run errands, or work out, you're continually programming yourself for success.

Great questioners are also great revenue generators and big income earners.

Do you sequentially and painstakingly ask each question? Of course not! Instead, your next question or series of questions is really dependent on your prospect's or customer's previous answers. Remember, the response to each question helps you develop your next question, so you can dig deeper and discover even more.

I kid clients (but they know it's true) that they could call me at 4:00 A.M., wake me from a sound sleep, and yell, "Go!" and I'd be able to rattle off a long list of open-ended need-development questions.

My goal is for you to do the same. (Although if you'd prefer, I'll buzz you during normal working hours!)

Profit Point

19

Ascend The Ladder.

One of the most valuable tools at your home or apartment is likely to be a ladder.

A ladder:

☆ Takes you to **new heights.**

☆ Helps you **reach places** you couldn't reach on your own.

☆ Takes you in **different directions.**

☆ Provides **support.**

☆ Lets you easily ascend or climb at your **own pace.**

☆ Gives you a **different perspective or viewpoint.**

☆ Takes you **to the top.**

It's for the same reasons The Ladder™ is also an extremely valuable strategy to have in your probe-and-prosper sales tool kit.

The Ladder is a transitional bridge from your initial contact with a customer, client, or prospect to the probing stage. The Ladder has been successfully used by my clients in a variety of industries—like financial services, distribution, and marketing. (As you'll soon see, it can be quickly, easily, and profitably adapted for you, too.)

To maximize your results, The Ladder simply needs to be planted, climbed, and extended. And that involves a six-step process.

The Ladder

Step 1
Plant the ladder:
with the help of The Fairness Doctrine.

Step 2
Climb the ladder:
with the use of transition language and open-ended need development questions.

Step 3
Continue to climb the ladder:
as you ask permission to take notes.

Step 4
Keep climbing the ladder:
with the use of support statements.

Step 5
Climb the ladder once again:
as you select and prioritize with clarification questions.

Step 6
Extend the ladder:
as you ask precommitment questions.

Step 1:
Plant the Ladder

You plant the ladder in Step 1 with some very powerful language. Here, you apply The Fairness Doctrine by saying:

> Would it be fair to say there are two things I already know about you?

1. "You're *serious* about money and your financial future." (Alternative words for financial could be business', family's, company's, etc.)

2. "It's important to you to make *sound* and *intelligent* financial decisions." (Alternative words for intelligent could be smart or wise.)

Get comfortable with this language. Repeat it several times. Alter your inflection. Change your intonation. Pause for effect. (For even more on The Fairness Doctrine, see Profit Pillar III.)

When on an actual sales call, be sure to let the power of these words sink in. Now you might be wondering, why is this initial "plant the ladder" language so effective? Here's why. Very early in the sales process with your customer, client, or prospect it establishes acknowledgment and purpose.

First, you acknowledge they're serious about money and their future. And second, you define the purpose of your meeting. You're focused on the importance of them making sound and intelligent financial, business, or family decisions. And *that* purpose is the same as yours. This mutual understanding lays the groundwork for a discussion or dialogue that's focused on results, not simply selling products or services.

Plus, it's hard for a prospect or customer to refute or disagree with your statements, since they logically reinforce positive attitudes and behaviors about money, investments, decisions, and results.

Once you have initial agreement from your prospect or client with your "plant the ladder" language, it's time to make a transition to a series of dramatic discovery or probing questions, so you can "climb the ladder."

Step 2:
Climb the Ladder

In Step 2, you use transition ladder language and ask intelligent questions about one's personal, family, or business issues, problems, challenges, goals, and dreams.

Here's sample transition ladder language:

"Ted, to help you, like I've helped other clients achieve their goals, I need to ask you a series of questions. First, let's focus on your personal goals."

Now, in this example, I would make a transition to questions of a personal nature to my prospect(s) or client(s). (Review your own list of questions, as well as the ones shared earlier in this Profit Pillar.)

As you know, there are literally hundreds of questions you can ask a prospect or client. However, don't be intimidated by the sheer volume of these questions. You're not expected to memorize or use all of them.

The real power of so many questions is you now have available lots to choose from. And choice is powerful. It allows you flexibility. And flexibility produces explosive results.

Step 3:
Climb the Ladder (with notes)

Be sure to ask permission to take notes.

Step 4:
Climb the Ladder (with support)

Now, in Step 4, you'll "climb the ladder" with some "support." Here are a variety of support statements. These are helpful and reassuring phrases you can use while your prospect or customer is responding and you're taking notes.

Potential support statements include:

☆ We're off to a great start.
☆ Excellent!
☆ That's helpful to know.

☆ Now, that's interesting.

☆ That's a unique viewpoint.

☆ That's a refreshing perspective.

☆ Wow! That's great!

☆ That's easy to understand.

☆ That's powerful!

☆ That's meaningful!

☆ That's significant!

☆ This is really good stuff!

☆ Tell me more.

☆ Please share more.

☆ I now have a better understanding.

☆ That gives me a deeper insight.

☆ That's strong!

☆ That's good to know.

☆ That's valuable.

☆ That's nice to hear.

☆ That makes sense.

Support statements are encouragers. Meaning, they encourage and positively prompt your prospects or clients to continue with their responses. They quickly realize while in your presence (or via the phone), there's a positive and free flow of information, especially when the content being provided is by and about them. After all, they're communicating about their favorite subject, themselves!

This simple process (that's positioned with The Ladder) immediately positions you in a unique and favorable way. For it's probably unlike any meeting or dialogue they've ever had with another sales professional.

They were likely preparing for and expecting a product pitch, info overload, or data dump. However, with the use of The Ladder and power probes, you provide neither. Instead, your sole focus is on their hopes, dreams, goals, and challenges. And with every response they make and support statement you make, you continually let them know how much you value and appreciate their participation and most important, *their story*.

Let's review a brief example of these first four steps in action. (We'll assume the meeting is taking place in the office of a financial adviser. Yet once again, the strategies are easily adaptable to you and your unique sales situation.)

In this scenario, look for the effective execution of the first four ladder steps:

1. Using the initial "plant the ladder" language.
2. Using the transition ladder language and then asking a series of open-ended need-development questions geared to one's personal life, personal problems, personal challenges, and personal goals. (Later we could focus on family and business issues, if appropriate.)
3. Asking permission to take notes.
4. Responding with support statements.

Here's The Ladder in action.

Success Scenario

Sales pro: Hi, Charlie, thanks for coming in. By us getting together today, would it be fair to say there are two things I already know about you?

1. You're *serious* about money and your financial future.
2. It's important to you to make *sound* and *intelligent* financial decisions.

Prospect: Yes, that's true.

Sales pro: Charlie, to help you, like I've helped other clients achieve their goals, I need to ask you a series of questions. First, let's focus on your personal goals.

Charlie, what matters most to you about money?

Prospect: That I have enough of it!

Sales pro: That makes sense. Tell me more. (Support statement.)

Prospect: (Charlie continues to wax rhapsodic.)

Sales pro: This is really good stuff. (Support statement.) Do you mind if I take notes?

Prospect: No, that's fine.

Sales pro: Charlie, what brings you the greatest happiness?

Prospect: Knowing both my family and business will prosper. (Charlie goes into detail. . . .)

Sales pro: Charlie, this is very helpful. (Support statement.)

Now let's imagine we walk out together into the future for five years. Tell me, Charlie, when you look back at that time, what would you have like to have accomplished?

Prospect: It would be really great when . . . (Charlie goes into more detail.)

The first four steps of The Ladder are really that easy. All you need to do is use:

1. Plant and transition ladder language.
2. Open-ended questions or power probes.
3. Note taking.
4. Support statements.

As you can tell, what makes this process so powerful is that the focus is on your prospect or customer and not on you, your company, your products, or your services.

Now, let's explore Step 5, clarification, and Step 6, precommitment.

Step 5:
Clarification

Let's imagine you have reached (based on your prospect or customer's responses) what seems like a logical conclusion to the questioning or probing phase. To confirm this, all you need to do is ask the clarification questions. These questions can include:

- ☆ "Anything else?"
- ☆ "What else would you like to share that'll help me or help you?"
- ☆ "Is there anything more important than what you've mentioned so far?"
- ☆ "What matters most on your (personal, business, family) list?"
- ☆ "How would you rank or prioritize these?"

Once you and your prospect or client have prioritized their personal, business, or family selections, it's time to extend the ladder with Step 6.

Step 6:
Precommitment

Here, you can use the extremely powerful precommitment question:

> "If we could develop (a written strategic program, a financial action plan, a game plan, a solution, a series of strategies, etc.) that would help you meet or exceed your goals (here, you reiterate their specific goals with their verbatim language that you began jotting down in Step 3), would that lay a strong foundation for us to work together?"

Now I realize this is a closed-ended or yea/nay question. But it's a really good one, because it generates early commitment or precommitment from your decision maker. They acknowledge that if you can help them meet or exceed their goals, the foundation is in place for your working relationship.

If in the unlikely event they say "No" you need to probe quickly to discover why they're hesitant. You might ask:

☆ "How come?"

☆ "Why do you feel that way?"

☆ "So I can best help you, please tell me about your concerns."

☆ "What else do we need to focus on, so we'll have a strong foundation for us to work together?"

(By the way no one, has ever told me "No" in response to the precommitment question.)

Once you get a thumbs-up to the precommitment question, consider saying and asking:

"Excellent! And, as we work together, today and for the long term, how should I share information with you?"

They might say, "Huh?" or "What do you mean?"

And your response is, "Well, I can be honest or diplomatic. Which do you prefer?"

Now the preceding may seem like a really strange question. But believe me, it's incredibly effective.

You, too, will soon discover that people always prefer for you to be honest. This enables you to share accurate, insightful, and perhaps even tough-to-hear info. (This also eliminates any attempt by your decision makers to "shoot the messenger" since they gave you the okay to give it to 'em straight.)

Let's quickly review why Steps 5 and 6, clarification and precommitment, are so important and so impactful.

In Step 5, when you seek clarification, it once again reinforces to your prospects or clients that these are the most important personal, business, or family issues, problems, and goals impacting their lives, today and in the future. The clarification further enables your customers to accept and acknowledge the challenges they may confront, as well as as the opportunities they may appreciate.

In Step 6, you seek the first of many commitments from your decision maker. This initial commitment helps set the stage for future commitments. That's why it's so important to ask the precommitment question:

"If we could develop (a written strategic program, a financial action plan, a game plan, a solution, a series of strategies, etc.) that would help you meet or exceed your goals (here, you reiterate their specific goals), would that lay a strong foundation for us to work together?"

This language is crucial. The words are very carefully selected.
Let's examine this language in order to understand its power.
First, "If we could develop a written strategic program . . ."
When something is in writing, it has substance. Meaning. Significance. And this is not simply a written program; it's a written strategic program. Strategy implies thought, brainpower, and analysis. (I realize your product or service might not rely on the written word to secure commitment, yet if it does, the preceding language really delivers.)

Next, we refer to "a financial action plan." A plan is like a blueprint or a road map. But an "action" plan also conveys movement, progress, and results. And that's what your decision makers crave: results! (You might create a "growth plan" or a "results plan" or a "performance plan.")

Next, we talk about helping one "meet or exceed your goals." Wow, now that's impactful! If you can help them meet their goals, you're talented. However, when you can help them exceed their goals, you quickly become a hero!

And finally, the language ". . . would that lay a strong foundation for us to work together?"

A strong foundation. That's obviously the best kind. For it conveys strength, stability, and reliability. And you stress that you and your prospect, client, or customer will be working together. You're like teammates or partners.

And it's for these reasons you want to use language like:

"If we could develop (a written strategic program, a financial action plan, a game plan, a solution, a series of strategies, etc.) that would help you meet or exceed your goals, would that lay a strong foundation for us to work together?"

Because when they say "Yes" to you here, early in the sales process, there's a far greater likelihood they'll say "Yes" to you later as well.

Remember, if they say "No" to you here, which is unlikely, at least you know this person is likely to remain a suspect and shouldn't be elevated to the status of a prospect.

Now, let's quickly explore part two of the precommitment language.

You state and ask . . .

"Excellent! And, as we work together, today and for the long term, how should I share information with you? I can be honest or diplomatic. Which do you prefer?"

The purpose of this question is to seek their okay for you to always be honest. On occasion, your business may require you to share some tough truths. However, honesty is essential for a successful relationship. It's nonnegotiable. Seeking and obtaining their approval to be honest allows you the comfort to always play it straight. And people actually respect you for it.

While clients have not always liked the information I've discovered about their organization, they've always been appreciative of the fact that I told them. Honesty and facts are the basis for successful relationships and intelligent decision making.

Remember . . .

The Ladder is a transitional bridge. It's strong, stable, and sturdy. It's on solid ground. It's firmly planted. It reduces risk. It offers safety. And it helps you take your prospects, customers, and clients closer to their goals.

Once again, one of the great values of this process is that it allows you and your prospect or customer to engage in a meaningful dialogue. And it's a dialogue you politely guide, as you skillfully probe and qualify.

As you'll soon discover, the entire question, qualify, probe, and ladder process will make your job infinitely easier. You'll find yourself having quicker and deeper insights into your prospects and decision makers. Any reluctance or hesitation will be replaced with comfort and candor.

Management guru Peter Drucker declared almost 50 years ago, "The only valid definition of business purpose is to create a satisfied customer."

The Ladder and power probes help you define and attain that satisfaction.

Drucker's axiom is timeless. It should be observed, internalized, and mastered. Then it'll pave the way to your more favorable and profitable future.

Climb the ladder. And ascend, my friend!

P.I.T. Stop

P   Provocative or Playful

I   Inspirational or Informational

T   Thoughts or Theories

Doughnut Delight

Best assumptive question I've ever heard:

"Welcome to Krispy Kreme, home of the fresh, hot, glazed doughnut. How many dozen would you like?"

Homework Horror!

Most baffling question from my son Chad's seventh-grade science book:

How does the wave model of electron placement differ from the model of electron position proposed by Niels Bohr?

Ummm! I think the correct answer is C!

Prescription for Success

Why is it, when you're young, you crave all-night restaurants and late-night bars? Yet as you get older, you desperately seek a 24-hour pharmacy?

> *"The art of learning is the art of reading with questions."*
> —*Sheldon Nahmod,*
> *one of my law school professors*

20

Yummy green bug juice!

A client recently asked, "Jeff, you always stress the value and significance of words and language. Is it really that big a deal?"

My response: "If you want long-term business-growth success, you bet! If instead you want a quick path to extinction, fuh-ged-uh-bout-it!"

Here are three examples.

Capture the Magic

While at O'Hare International Airport, I overheard one businessman say to another, "What should I say? Can you give me magic words?"

This fellow was searching for words of wisdom. He wanted to avoid language losers. Why? Because the words, phrases, and questions you use really do matter! Especially in a sales, marketing service, or persuasive message.

This point was driven home by a bunch of first graders!

Nobody Wants Citrus Cooler

When we celebrated our youngest child Amanda's seventh birthday in her school classroom, my wife served chocolate cupcakes, while Brittany, our other daughter, and I were in charge of "drink distribution."

To the first group of four kids I asked, "Would you like apple juice or citrus cooler?" Each, with a look of confusion, cautiously responded, "Apple juice."

Brittany said, "Daddy, nobody wants citrus cooler."

Boom! It hit me!

I exclaimed, "Brittany, how could they? Why would they? Who the heck even knows what citrus cooler is?! I used ill-conceived language that didn't appeal to their dominant buying motives for risk, excitement, and adventure."

Brittany then said what she often says: "Daddy, you're very strange!"

I said, "Brit, watch this!" I then asked 15 more children, "Which would you like—regular apple juice or yummy green bug juice?"

Their eyes bulged! Cheeks puffed! Smiles erupted! And 14 of 15 exclaimed, "Gimme yummy green bug juice!"

Gus' Gaffe

Gus, a salesperson for a personal-improvement web site, was trying to woo me to advertise on his site. In his voice-mail messages he assured me, "Jeff, you'll make big bucks just like your friends in the industry." I was skeptical, but set up a brief phone meeting. We scheduled a time and date for Gus to reach me on my private line.

Gus called—20 hours early!

I told him I was chatting with a client on another line and could he please call back at the scheduled time. He said dejectedly, "Okay, I was just hoping to pitch you now." (Hmmm. He wasn't going to assess my goals and needs, he was "pitching.")

The next day, I waited for the phone to ring. It didn't. Gus blew off our phone date.

Ninety minutes later, my private line rang. It was Gus. I asked, "Gus, is everything okay? I expected your call at two o'clock."

He replied, "Oh, I didn't call because we're moving our offices and I lost track of time." (Gus sells self-improvement and he can't keep track of time!)

He then said, "Let's make this quick. This will work for you. You deserve to pay $600."

I exclaimed, "I 'deserve to pay'?"

He said, "Ummm, maybe that's not the right word." (No kidding!)

Gus then tried to flatter me when he boldly declared, "Jeff, I've already gotten commitments from other superstars like you. (It didn't work. I'm not a big fan of fawning and insincere praise.)

When I asked, "Who?" He started name-dropping. (Amazingly, every name he dropped he mispronounced!)

I politely ended the conversation by requesting he send me this "superstars" list so I could confirm their results. He assured me, "You'll get it today."

I never did.

Power Words and Profit Phrases

I've actually created a list of 189 power words and profit phrases. Here's a sneak preview of 51 of them:

Proven	Partnership	Lightest
New	Bargain	Compact
Research	Exclusive	Prestige
Priceless	Free	Craftsmanship
Trouble free	Investment	Solid
Biggest	Quality	Contemporary
Reliable	First	Safety
Savings	Bandwagon	Service
Sound	Special offer	No extra cost
Effortlessly	Value	Superior
Reputation	Flexible	Natural
Responsible	European	Big selection
Multifaceted	Accurate	Quick
Seamless	Can't resist	Beautiful

Classic	Invisible	Best
Preference	Special finish	Longevity
Richness	Modular	Peace of mind

Would you like to see the complete list?
For *free*? Of course you would! Simply . . .

send an e-mail to: jeff@jeffblackman.com with the subject heading:

Hey Gus, Buy a Clue!

and we'll send you a copy via e-mail.

Here's to winning words on your path to profit!

Profit Point

21

Gotcha!

Once I was lured into a men's clothing store by a large sign:

Bargain! We Won't Be Undersold! Sale Today!

While sifting through suits, I heard a salesman exclaim to his customer who just bought one suit, "As long as I got you in a buying mood, I'll take advantage of it!"

The ignorance of his statement caused me to grab for pen and paper, record his "classic sales motivator," and send it to the Museum of Stupid Business History!

Let's analyze this myopic marketeer's not-so-clever come-on:

"As long as I got you"

Although a fine haberdasher attempts to fit a man's entire body, this statement seemingly indicates the salesman may have "gotten" his customer by another part of his anatomy!

"in a buying mood"

Are we ever in a "buying mood"? Sure! But what does that really mean? The mood of the new clothes shopper is often pride, recognition, and status. This shopper isn't just buying clothes; he or she is investing in enhanced self-image. Products and services must be marketed and sold with emotion, yet rationalized with logic!

"I'll take advantage of it!"

This salesman was already counting his commission! His focus was on *his* paycheck, not his *customer's* satisfaction. He was pushing clothes—not value, pride, self-esteem, and quality.

He may have cleaned up with this customer, but long-term, he's programmed for failure! With a value-driven, integrity-based, and nonmanipulative approach, he might have asked, "With the biggest savings of the year, how would *you* like to take advantage of . . . ?"

Remember, one foolish utterance often destroys the rapport and trust of your business relationship. It's better for people to think you're a fool than to open your mouth and confirm it!

Profit Point

22

Move your world.

Joseph Conrad once said,

> **"If you give me the right word and the correct accent
> in which to speak it . . . I can move the world."**

And he's right!

Words are powerful stuff. They stir emotion. They create action. They can motivate the masses to produce remarkable results. Yet they can also incite battles, riots, and wars—and, of course, blow business opportunities!

Words intrigue me. The right word or combination of words makes things happen. Fast!

> **With words, you can leverage language, create
> profit phrases, position perception, or discover
> unique ways to probe and prosper.**

Here are five powerful examples:

1. Emotion and logic in action.

Saab, the Swedish auto manufacturer, once ran two full-page ads side by side in business magazines. The headline of the left-hand page read, "21 Logical Reasons to Buy a Saab." This headline was followed by 21 logical reasons, such as four-valve technology, advanced ergonomics, or a special steel underpanel. (This page was in black and white.)

The headline of the right-hand page had three simple words: "One Emotional Reason!" Beneath this headline was a color picture of a Saab Turbo blurring through the countryside.

Wow! Talk about impact! It delivered features logically, in black and white, and then stressed emotionally, in living color, that the Saab driving experience is about speed, satisfaction, and style.

Your sales and marketing messages—in person, over the phone, or via your ads, brochure, web site, or even written correspondence—must convey the right perception, emotion, attitude, cadence, and content. These subtleties maximize impact, value, results, and profits!

2. Smart art.

As my wife and I entered an art gallery, the owner asked, "Wouldn't that painting look better on your wall than on mine?"

3. A winning warning.

Many signs say: *Children must be accompanied by an adult.* However, in Michigan City, Indiana, a sign declared:

Now is a good time . . . to take your child by the hand.

Enjoy your visit!

4. Moral hygiene.

My dental hygienist, Sue Argo, knew it would be tough to berate me about forgetful flossing, so instead she said, "Jeff, since you own your own business, how would you feel if I could share with you a strategy that will leave thousands of dollars in your pocket?"

5. Cheese to please.

From the cover of a Viccinos pizza box:

Life is short. Go gourmet!

Love that line! Only five words, but in a whimsical way it empha-sizes quality, value, and indulgence. (And it works. Big time! My family and I have the empty pizza boxes to prove it!)

Here are more profit-producing language upgrades:

Do not write proposals.
Instead, create action plans.

Do not have contracts with terms.
Instead, have agreements with requests.

Do not demand a down payment.
Instead, request an initial investment.

Do not give discounts.
Instead, consider offering economic concessions or courtesy sav-ings, yet only when you get something in return.

And be sure to knock out these language losers:

Let me be frank . . .
To be honest with you . . .
I'd like to be candid . . .
I'm going to tell you straight . . .
I say this sincerely . . .

Huh?
With the preceding, does it mean if somebody doesn't give you a heads-up, then they're not frank, not honest, not candid, not straight, and not sincere?!

Profit Point

23

A tip from Down Under.

Australians have introduced us to Crocodile Dundee, shrimp on the barbie, and Vegemite sandwiches. However, they're especially proud of their native invention, the boomerang!

What happens when you toss a boomerang? That's correct: It comes right back to you. This action also makes the "boomerang" a potent and powerful sales strategy.

How would you respond to somebody who asks, "Is that a popular selling product?" If you're like most salespeople, you'd probably state in a confident and commanding voice, "You bet it's popular, one of our best sellers!" Their retort might be, "Oh, that's too bad. I wanted something really special and unique! Something my friends don't have!" If so, you're sunk! And it's unlikely you'll recover.

However, let's examine this same scenario with the use of the "boomerang." When the customer inquires, "Is that a popular selling product?" Your response should be, "Is popularity important to you?" or "Are you looking for something that many others have?" or "Do you want something unique?"

When the customer now indicates his or her desire for that one-of-a-kind or unique product, you continue to probe, to uncover what "one-of-a-kind" means, what the customer envisions or hopes to accomplish.

The boomerang gets your decision maker
logically and emotionally involved.

The "boomerang" applies to a variety of situations. For example, how would you now respond to somebody who inquires . . .

"How often will I hear from you?"
("How often would you like to hear from me?")

"What type of warranty do you have?"
("What type are you most interested in?")

"Are there others I can talk to whom you have helped?"
("Absolutely. How many would you like to contact?")

Now, I know what you're thinking: This is a drawn-out and repetitive approach. Sure, it requires another question, but it's a question that elicits a response from your customer's perspective. There's a big difference between you saying, "This strategy or solution offers . . ." and your prospect or customer stating, "I need a strategy that does . . ."

Toss It One More Time

I'll never forget a conversation I had with the president of a large and successful insurance agency. During our first meeting he asked, "Jeff, who on my team should attend your series of skill-building programs?" I started to respond, "Well, there are a couple of possibilities—" but then interrupted myself and asked, "Milt, who do you think should be there and would benefit the most?" He replied, "I want the rookies to show up, because they're young, hungry, and excited. They're the new blood, our future. But I also want some of the veterans there. They're smart, still competitive, and they've got great war stories to tell!" I told Milt that made a lot of sense.

He then asked, "Jeff, what do we highlight first?" I paused, glanced at my notes in a moment of reflection, looked up, and said, "Hmmm, Milt, what do *you* think we should highlight first?" He told me. For the next five minutes!

Then he asked, "Jeff, if there's one skill you think is important for my people to master as a result of your sessions, what would that be?" I pondered his question and thoughtfully replied, "Milt, that depends. What would you like it to be?" He then made an emphatic statement I'll never forget: "Jeff, I'd consider this program to be an incredible success if my people could just learn how to answer a question with a question!" I smiled and said, "Milt, why is that skill so important to you?" And of course, he told me!

I had repeatedly "boomeranged" Milt. But why was he willing to always respond? Simple. He was logically and emotionally involved. He knew the motivation for my words and questions was to help, not to harass. They were designed to discover, not to disturb.

Profit Point

24

The Fairness Doctrine.

Have you ever been in a sales interview when you're suddenly confronted by some seemingly insurmountable dilemma, like the loyalty barrier. You know how that one goes:

You're finally in front of prospects Mr. and Ms. I'm Not Gonna Budge. You've made previous contact with the Budges—17 times by phone, fax, e-mail, and mail—and now they have granted you only 15 minutes. Unfortunately, within the first five minutes, they let you know you're wasting your time because your number one competitor, Hard Sell Enterprises, to whom they're very loyal, has been taking care of them for 20 years and they're not about to change now!

At this point, many salespeople would dejectedly pack up and leave. Others would try to convince Mr. or Ms. I'm Not Gonna Budge as to why switching to their company, product, or service makes more sense. This latter strategy is also a loser. Why? Because the more you try to convince the Budges to budge, they'll defiantly and stubbornly hold their ground.

Prospects don't like to be told how stupid their previous decisions were.

The harder you sell, the stronger their resistance. So what do you do? Easy. Apply The Fairness Doctrine. Here's how it works. Ask the Budges a series of very specific questions. For example:

☆ What do they like best about their current supplier?
☆ How has the supplier helped them?
☆ What benefits do the supplier's products deliver?

While your prospects enthusiastically tell you all the reasons they're happy, loyal, satisfied, and not about to budge, you listen patiently and intently. When they're done, you briefly summarize the key points they just mentioned. For example, you might say, "I can now understand why you've been so happy with Hard Sell Enterprises. The things especially important to you are their quality, on-time delivery, and follow-up." Your prospects or suspects are of course nodding their heads in agreement, confident you've been defeated and you'll now bolt for an escape route. However, now you apply The Fairness Doctrine.

You simply ask the Budges a question that begins with these six words:

"Would it be fair to say . . ."

For example,

"Would it be fair to say that even if we could provide you with quality, on-time deliveries, and follow-through that were as good as or even better than Hard Sell Enterprises provides, you still wouldn't want to discuss it? Would it be fair to say that?"

Now you wait. And if they say, "Yes, it would be fair to say that," you now know they're unwilling to listen, change, alter, or budge. To this prospect you say adios, *sayonara*, *arrivederci*, ciao, shalom, I'm outta here, 'bye! Why? Because your wise words and power probes can't turn this suspect into a prospect.

What's the real value of The Fairness Doctrine and the "would it be fair to say" question?

The Fairness Doctrine lets your prospect know you're willing to leave. Your precious time, effort, and energy will no longer be devoted (at least for now) to this particular prospect.

However, before you leave, there are still several key things for you to say and ask. Now remember, I'll never share with you any strategy, tip, or technique unless I myself do it and have had success with it. Therefore, when I have unfortunately discovered I'm still dealing with a suspect and not a prospect, I'll say something like,

"Phil, it's too bad we won't have the opportunity to work together now, but would it be fair to say that what you're really telling me is not 'no' but instead 'not yet'?"

At this point, Phil will usually smile and say something like, "I'd be more than happy, Jeff, to visit again. Call me in three months." I of course make a note to follow up, but then I ask Phil one more question before I go.

I might say, "Phil, just out of curiosity, who else do you know, obviously noncompetitive, who could benefit from our profit-producing business-growth strategies?"

Now usually one of three things can happen.

The exception is for them to say things like, "Well, I'm not a very good networker," "I don't get out much," or "I have no idea." I assure you, responses like this are not the norm.

Second, they might say something like, "Let me think about it. Call me next week, I'll have some names." Believe it or not, when I call them next week, they really *do* have a bunch of names.

And finally, the most common result is that after I ask, "Phil, just out of curiosity, who else do you know, obviously noncompetitive, who could benefit from our profit-producing business-growth strategies?" something interesting happens. Immediately Phil starts to flip through his actual or mental Rolodex or database and he begins to give me names and numbers. This simple strategy has helped me discover countless new prospects who became clients.

The reason that this strategy works is psyche—my psyche, as well as the referral source's psyche. I didn't say, "Could you give me a lead?" or "Would you recommend me in the future?" or "How about passing out a few of my business cards?" Instead, I asked who they knew that I could help or who could benefit from what I do. This simple repositioning of the question quickly leads to results.

And here's what I think happens with the referral source's psyche. Most people find it difficult to say "no" or for that matter even "not yet." They feel guilty, as if they've rejected you. Therefore, in an attempt to remove their guilt, they'll be helpful and accommodate your request.

(For a boatload of referral strategies, see Profit Pillar VI: Referrals: Your Road to Results!®)

The Fairness Doctrine with a Dose of Change

Let's see what happens with The Fairness Doctrine when your prospect is now willing to listen or at least consider a potential change.

Remember, you ask the question:

"Would it be fair to say that even if we could provide you with quality, on-time deliveries, and follow-through that were as good as or even better than Hard Sell Enterprises provides, you still wouldn't want to discuss it? Would it be fair to say that?"

This time they say, "No, it wouldn't be fair to say that! If you could do those things better or faster than Hard Sell, I'd at least be willing to listen!" Perfect. That's the response you've been waiting for. Now you begin to probe even deeper to discover what they really want to accomplish, do different, or do better.

When you apply The Fairness Doctrine with the phrase, "Would it be fair to say," the results are rapid and significant. Your "no budge" prospect opens your door to opportunity. And the potential for that opportunity, for you and for them, is achieved with winning words in a question, not a statement.

Profit Point

25

A piece of the pie.

How'd you like to replace or eliminate your competitors? Cool! But unlikely. Because as we've already determined, buyers are reluctant to change, even if the change helps them attain a more favorable future. Therefore, as much as you'd like to replace your competitors, your decision makers will have a comfort or security level with the past they probably won't want to disrupt.

My suggestion is never try to replace your competitor. Instead, position yourself to become the next best solution. Here's the question you ask:

> "Irv, I can now understand why you've been so happy with Hard Sell Enterprises and why you wouldn't want to replace them. So let me ask you this: How can I (our company and our products and services) complement what Hard Sell is doing for you?"

This question is extremely powerful. Here's why: It allows your decision maker to breathe a sigh of relief. He now knows he doesn't have to replace his current supplier. There could be high risk with replacement, but minimal risk when he complements. Together, you and your decision maker can now determine how you can complement, contribute to, or be a part of his solution, and not the entire solution. (If you can't get the whole pie, be sure to get a tasty slice of it!)

Profit Point

26

The Blue Suit.

A blue suit is considered traditional or conservative. And for The Blue Suit strategy to work, *conservative* (or *conservatively*) becomes the operative word. This approach is disarmingly simple, but incredibly effective. Here's how it works.

Whatever your product or service, it's probably designed to in some way maximize gain and/or minimize loss. No matter what product or service you're selling, the application of The Blue Suit is essentially the same. Here's how I apply it in my business.

My clients depend on me to be a business-growth specialist. I help them improve the performance, productivity, and profitability of their people and company in a variety of ways: speaking, training, coaching, consulting, and business-growth tools. However, before I can help them grow and prosper from new sales, marketing, customer service, leadership, or negotiation strategies, I must know what they perceive they're losing or not gaining because they don't have these skills or knowledge.

Therefore, here are the questions I might ask a potential client:

"Conservatively, as result of your sales team not having the negotiating skills you'd like, how much money are they leaving on the table?"

or,

> "If your people knew how to better prospect and manage their time and territory, **conservatively**, how many more dollars could they generate?"

You might apply The Blue Suit by asking "conservatively" questions linked to:

- ☆ Time.
- ☆ Convenience.
- ☆ Dollars.
- ☆ Productivity.
- ☆ Performance.
- ☆ Profitability.

For example:

> **"Conservatively, how many opportunities or dollars are being lost** because you're not investing, as you said, the way you'd like to?"

or,

> **"Conservatively, how much time are you devoting** to repairs? And what's the **conservative economic impact** on productivity and profitability?"

Your creative adaptation and use of the conservative Blue Suit strategy will have quick and dramatic results.

Find the Pain

Once I applied The Blue Suit in this way with a potential client. I asked,

> "By your own admission, you're not effectively using your referral sources. Because of that, conservatively, how much in annual revenues are you losing?"

The president of the company paused, and then in an exasperated tone mumbled, "Probably a hundred million dollars a year."

I gasped and said, "A hundred million dollars a year? Are you serious?!" He reluctantly nodded his head. Then his vice president exclaimed, "No way!" The president said, "What, do you think it's less?" To which the VP said, "No. It's higher—closer to $125 million!"

I gasped again and said, "A hundred twenty-five million dollars a year? Are you kidding?!" The VP said, "Let me explain."

He then told me in great detail about all of the opportunities they had blown. The president sat silent, but was nodding his head in frustrated agreement. The power of this question is that my prospects quantified their pain! They assigned a numerical and tangible dollar sign to their suffering.

By the way, once that dollar figure is given, you have to show almost physical disbelief. If you recall, I responded with surprise and amazement, then asked, "Are you serious?" "Are you kidding?"

Here's one more subtlety to The Blue Suit. Once their dollar figure of anguish is shared, and you have expressed your surprise, ask this question:

"Mr. Prospect, if you had that extra $125 million, what would you do with it?"

Now, they begin to plan, dream, and visualize for you. My prospects began to talk about return on investment, expansion, new market penetration, and enhanced growth. They freely expressed their aches and pains and then wanted to know how I could rid them of their ailments and make them well!

By using The Blue Suit, how many more people will you help attain a more favorable future? And conservatively, how many more dollars, sales, and earnings will that mean to you?

Profit Point

27

Budget builders.

At what stage of the sales process do you determine or gain some insight into your decision maker's budget? That's right—it's done early, with winning words that are part of the probe. Because not only must your prospects and customers have a need to fill, dream to realize, or problem to solve, but they must also have the ability to pay for it!

You should never place yourself in a position to guess at somebody else's budget or investment potential. "Budget builder" questions remove the guesswork and uncertainty. However, your decision maker may be unwilling to share with you a budget or a number, or may say something like:

☆ "I have no idea what this should cost; that's why I called you!"

☆ "Money is no object. If it's worth it, I'll pay it!"

If you get responses like these, you can still determine the budget. Here's one way. You let your buyer know you want them to make the best possible decision. And that decision will obviously be a reflection of their goals, needs, and budget.

Therefore, if they have no idea what the investment might be, you can share several ranges. For example, you let them know other satisfied clients or customers with similar predicaments, dilemmas, or goals have invested within three ranges. Let's say:

Range 1 is $5,000 to $10,000.

Range 2 is $11,000 to $20,000.

Range 3 is $21,000 or greater.

(In this example, the principles matter, not the dollar amounts. Simply apply the figures most appropriate for you.) It's also important to stress that you should never put an ending parameter or restriction on your final range.

You now ask your decision maker, "Which range are you most comfortable with—1, 2, or 3?" If they say, "Range 2," you say, "Wonderful." You can even ask, "Would you prefer to stay closer to $11,000 or $20,000?" Their responses help guide you in your creation of the best possible solution.

Is the Budget Really Firm?

How do you handle the decision maker who gives you a "firm" budget?

Let's take a look at an example that's easy to relate to. Imagine I'm a real estate agent and you're a motivated buyer. We've already determined you want a four-bedroom, two-and-a-half-bath house in a quiet community, close to schools, shopping, and transportation, and the lot has to be at least a quarter of an acre. You have told me you're only willing to look at homes listed at $350,000 or less.

Suppose, armed with this information, I first take you to a house listed at $375,000. Not only do you detest the floor plan and neighborhood, but you're also disappointed and disturbed with me, because the house was listed at more than $350,000. You feel I took you here just so I'd make more on my commission! Uh-oh. I'm in trouble! You feel I didn't listen, and you may begin to question my integrity.

However, what if this next scenario took place? Imagine I said to you,

"Let's make sure I understand what's important to you. You'd like a four-bedroom, two-and-a-half-bath house in a quiet community, close to schools, shopping, and transportation, and the lot has to be at least a quarter of an acre. You have also told me you're only willing to look at homes listed at $350,000 or less, correct?"

You nod affirmatively.

Now I ask a question that combines the budget builder strategy along with The Fairness Doctrine:

> "If I come across a listing that offers you and your family
> everything you want—the space, the community, the lot size,
> and then some—but it's listed at more than $350,000, would
> it be fair to say you'd prefer I not even show it to you?"

Now how do you think you'd react? It's likely you'll say, "Well, if it had all that, I guess I'd be willing to look at it." I say, "Great! How much more than $350,000 are you comfortable with?" You say, "Up to $380,000 is probably okay, maybe even $400,000, but then it has to be something really special!"

Who just increased the budget? Me or you? You did! And it was accomplished once again with winning words in a power probe.

Profit Point

28

Total satisfaction.

Prospects and customers can be very clever about the creative ways they delay decisions. They're hesitant about offending you with a defiant "No!" so instead they say things like:

☆ "I'd like to think it over!"

☆ "Boy, it sounds interesting!"

☆ "We'll give it our top consideration!"

☆ "It looks real promising!"

☆ "I'll be sure to put in a good word for you!"

☆ "This looks like a real strong possibility!"

☆ "It'll require some careful thought!"

☆ "Everything sure seems to be in order!"

☆ "You've done a great job presenting this!"

☆ "We'll get back to you as soon as possible!"

☆ "I think we might, could, perhaps, maybe . . . be able to do it!"

☆ "Just as soon as we've made up our minds . . . you'll be the first to know!"

Do these stall tactics sound familiar?

Thought so. But what do they mean? Who knows? I've got no idea! Therefore, you must find out what's causing the hesitation and reluctance.

If you allow your customers to escape without knowing what's causing their indecision, *you* haven't done *your* job! You must determine the reason(s) for their unwillingness to say "Yes!" now.

Dig for Doubt

If customers tell you, "I'd like to think it over," don't argue with them. Instead, acknowledge you understand their desire to think it over. After all, it *is* an important decision. But then discover *what* they'd really like to think over. You might say,

"What specifically would you like to think about?" (And after the answer, ask, "In addition to that, is there anything else?")

Once you've isolated the obstacle, you're then in a better position to respond, reassure, and get a "yes" decision. You should try to never exit without knowing why a customer hasn't yet invested or said "yes." If you do, you're no longer relying on knowledge, but instead on guesswork.

Another successful strategy for the decision-delayer "I'd like to think it over" is:

> "I can understand why you'd like to think it over. It *is* an important decision. Let's list the points you'd like to consider. . . . Any others?"

The decision delayers can even be written down—by *you*, not your customer. Then you might say,

> "If I could answer or address these points to your *total satisfaction*—would you be ready to go ahead with your decision?"

Or:

> "If I could resolve these issues to your *total satisfaction*, would you be ready to approve this action plan?"

Or:

> "If you're not comfortable, I'm not comfortable. Therefore, if together we can eliminate your concerns to your *total satisfaction*, would you then be willing to give this idea your approval?"

There are two important keys to this very effective strategy. First, your customer knows her concerns must be answered to her "total satisfaction"; and second, once these concerns are answered, she should then be ready, willing, and able to give you a "yes." Once again, the concept is crucial. Therefore, aside from saying, "If I can address these points to your total satisfaction . . ." you might say:

> "If I can address these issues and remove your doubt . . ."

Or:

"If we explore the choices so you're completely comfortable . . ."

Or:

"Your unconditional satisfaction is essential. Together, let's see how we can help you achieve that."

Here's an important subtlety to this strategy. If you've written down your customer's concerns, then once each point is properly answered or addressed, cross it off! This shows tangible evidence that one by one, the customer's objections, hesitancies, and decision delayers are being eliminated. And with the elimination of each point, you move closer to a "yes."

By using such language, your focus is not on a slick comeback to an objection, but instead on your prospect's real concerns and total satisfaction or complete comfort. And that's where your focus belongs.

This is no time to engage in a tug-of-war or battle of wits. If you do, you're likely to defeat yourself. But . . .

**When your decision maker perceives and experiences
a cooperative, problem-solving,
satisfaction-producing scenario, they're willing
to work *with* you, not against you.**

Profit Point

29

Objection overruled.

The winner of the worst response to a simple objection is:

> **Telemarketer:** "The reason I'm calling is to send you information on our new credit card."
>
> **Me:** "Not necessary, but that was nice of you to call."
>
> **His response:** A long sigh. A loud "Ugh!" An audible moan. And then, he hung up.

Not exactly what you'd call a snappy comeback. And what's mind-boggling is I can't imagine he hadn't heard this objection before.

**Objections shouldn't terminate dialogue;
they should help promote it.**
**They're really nothing more than a delay,
a tangent, or even a couched inquiry for more information.**

I'm convinced prospects and customers often toss out objections just to see what the responses might be.

Objections are easy to combat when you're ready for them. So to be prepared instead of perplexed. Realize . . .

Objections (of any kind) usually fall into one of four categories:

1. No bucks.
2. No desire.
3. No immediacy.
4. No belief.

If your decision maker claims they've got no bucks, focus on quality, value, and return on investment.

If your decision maker has no desire, probe. Then probe some more. Search for problems to solve, needs to fill, and dreams or goals to realize.

If your decision maker has no immediacy, help them answer the question, "How does time become your enemy if you choose to do nothing?"

If your decision maker has no belief, it means they have skepticism about you, your company, your product, or your service. To instill confidence and faith, offer:

☆ Proof   ☆ Comparative analysis
☆ Testimonials   ☆ Exhibits
☆ Analogies   ☆ Success stories
☆ Case studies   ☆ Research
☆ Demonstrations   ☆ Statistics

"Obstacles and objections are like wild animals. They're cowards. They'll bluff you if they can. If they see you're afraid, they're likely to pounce upon you. So instead, look 'em squarely in the eye, and watch 'em slink out of sight."

—*Orison Swett Marden*

Objections are a traditional part of the sales process. But often they're created by the seller, not the buyer. Therefore, conceptually there's no need to learn how to handle them if they never exist. While I'll still share with you strategies to overcome them, ideally my suggestion is for you to simply avoid them.

The best objection is the one you never get!

Objection avoidance is far more powerful than objection handling. (Yet this can be achieved only with winning words, great power probes, and your strong conveyance of value, early and throughout the sales process.)

A client once asked me, "Jeff, don't lots of objections show strong signs of buyer interest?" Unfortunately, no. They show strong signs of buyer resistance. Objections aren't necessarily "camouflaged opportunities." They represent buyer barriers. These barriers can be avoided, prevented, and precluded by you when your total focus is on helping your decision maker solve a problem, fulfill a need, or realize a goal.

Despite your best efforts, though, on occasion an obstacle or objection might still sneak its way into your world. If that does happen, no worries. Simply "go A.P.E."!

Profit Point

30

Go A.P.E.

I often suggest to clients that to combat an obstacle or objection they should "go A.P.E."

Meaning:

Anticipate.

Plan.

Execute.

Anticipate

Anticipate is easy, because you're likely hearing the same objections repeatedly. They probably deal with issues or concerns regarding price, performance, quality, delivery, previous or current relationships, service, image, reputation, culture, or risk.

For example:

- ☆ That's more than I wanted to spend.

- ☆ Your price is a lot higher than others'.

- ☆ It's too expensive.

- ☆ I'd like to think it over.

- ☆ We're too busy, we've got no time to meet.

- ☆ We're happy with our current supplier.

- ☆ We've really got no need.

- ☆ We tried that once, but it didn't work.

- ☆ Need to talk to my partner. She'll be back in five years.

- ☆ Okay, I'll do it, but you have to reduce the price.

- ☆ We can get it cheaper.

- ☆ We have no budget.

- ☆ Our budget is all used up.

- ☆ What if it doesn't work?

- ☆ That'll never work!

- ☆ What do the studies show?

- ☆ That'll take too long.

- ☆ There's no need to make a change.

- ☆ I'm happy with your competitor.

- ☆ I'm afraid it won't be here in time.

☆ What if you're out of stock?

☆ You're too big for us!

☆ You're too small for us!

☆ We don't need you; we can do it ourselves.

☆ Changing would be such a hassle.

☆ You don't offer anything different or unique.

☆ I'm really just looking.

☆ Nobody would use it!

☆ We can't make any decision without the approval of the board, the committee, the council, our attorney, or accountant.

☆ Our people would be scared of doing something new.

☆ Call me when the economy is better.

☆ We'd like to pay with a credit card, plus net 90 days!

☆ Why aren't you certified?

Have you heard one or more of the preceding? Yep. Thought so.
As you can see, these (and most) objections or obstacles are ones of:

☆ **Delay:** "I'd like to think it over."

☆ **Denial:** "Nobody would use it."

☆ **Distrust:** "You don't offer anything different or unique."

Before you decide how you'll combat an objection, determine how you'll first combat yourself. Huh? (For example, if you're repeatedly getting premature price objections, discover why. Perhaps you're too quick to give an information and feature dump before effectively probing. Or you mistakenly keep stressing you charge less than your competitors, which draws attention to price, not value.) Here, an objection is likely to be the result of *your* wrong behavior. Sorry, but it's likely *you're* the reason for the objection, not your buyer.

Therefore, let's focus on the right behavior when an objection pops up.

You can always try to combat objections or obstacles with facts, logic, data, surveys, and statistics. These help. They're a great place to start. However, you had better also appeal to the decision maker's "perceived reality"—meaning what their gut tells them is the issue or concern. And you accomplish this with "persuasive emotion."

> *"One who attempts to move people to thought or action must concern himself with their emotions. If he touches only their minds, he is unlikely to move them to action or to change of mind—the motivations of which lie deep in the realm of the passions."*
>
> —*Aristotle*

Hey, I'll never downplay the significance of facts and logic. They're invaluable. But they don't always lead to a sale. With "persuasive emotion" you creatively focus on the buyer's inner feelings, concerns, needs, and motivators.

When you do this, you capture and tap into what movie character Austin Powers calls "Mo Jo."

Mo Jo is a special blend of power, energy, force, and momentum. It does more than merely adeptly deflect an objection or obstacle. It also conveys with clarity and conviction your unequivocal desire to help your decision maker make the right choice and do the right thing.

☆ **It's about the pursuit of your customer's goals, before the pursuit of your profit.**
☆ **It's about gaining the customer's commitment, not just their cash.**
☆ **It's about long-term results, not short-term conquests.**

You must create an environment with your responses so your decision makers know they can rely on and trust you.

The mind of the buyer can be a complex combination of fear, concern, and hesitation. Your job is to bust through this complexity with articulate, risk-reducing replies. You provide the types of answers that demonstrate both good business sense and intuitive emotional understanding.

This can only happen when you plan and take control.

Plan

Please grab another sheet of paper and make a list of your most frequent objections. Write them down. Now.

> *"Immense power is acquired by assuring yourself in your silent reveries that you were born to control affairs."*
>
> —*Andrew Carnegie*

Next, write word-for-word how you might respond. Write fast. Don't worry about perfection, yet. First, focus on creation. The key is to simply commit your ideas and potential responses to paper. Now, it's time to see if your new language works.

Execute

Start to experiment. Rehearse your new "success scripts" out loud. Record them. Listen back. Study. Practice. Practice some more.

How do they sound? Where can you change a word or a phrase? How about your inflection, pacing, or volume to make it more impactful?

Now it's the time for truth. When an obstacle or objection is launched in your direction, respond with the reply you've practiced.

See what needs to be upgraded or improved. Or have you found a winner? If so, excellent. Master it. Continue to use it.

Here are several objections or obstacles and possible responses. While you might be able to use the following replies, don't get hung up on the language. Instead, study the principles and rationales for these answers.

The 13 driving principles for responding to an objection or obstacle are:

1. Be respectful.
2. Be diplomatic.
3. Be empathetic.
4. Approach and welcome obstacles or objections with a positive attitude.
5. Acknowledge that obstacles or objections may give you valuable insight into the buyer's thought process.
6. Listen.
7. Focus on benefits and advantages.
8. Ask questions that help the decision maker realize it's risky, ineffective, or imprudent to move forward without your product or service.
9. Paraphrase or summarize the buyer's expressed reluctance or concern.
10. Use language that hits at both logical and emotional levels.
11. Always stress value.
12. Realize that the purpose of your response is not to make a sale; it's to get the buyer closer to the achievement of his or her goals. (By the way, when you do this, you make the sale!)
13. Know that the best way to overcome an objection is to never get one. Continually develop your skills to achieve "objection avoidance."

Understanding these principles, along with your ability and adaptability to skillfully apply them, will serve you far better than merely attempting to memorize the specific words you see in the following pages.

There's a big difference between parroting my words or somebody else's prose versus creating your own. Initially, let my words simply be the impetus or motivation for your multiple masterpieces!

Here are some likely objections or obstacles and possible replies or success scripts:

Objection or obstacle:
"We can get it for $10,000 less."

Potential success script:
Consider . . .

> "You're right, you probably could get it for less. Yet how would you feel if you spent a few dollars less and got the wrong results? What looks like an initial savings now could really become an expensive and painful cost later, in terms of time, energy, and money."
>
> "The results strategies we'll implement together are all within the budget ranges we previously discussed. And most important, investing only a few more dollars assures you the right results, so it really becomes a bargain."
>
> "As you said, the key benefits and real value are . . ."
>
> "And what positive impact would that have on . . . ?"

Objection or obstacle:
"Hi, my name is Dana from Wonder Widgets, and I'm the assistant to our president, Joshua David. He asked me to find out about your products and services. Please send us some information along with your prices."

Potential success script:
Consider . . .

> "Dana, sure appreciate your call."

Then, ask questions like . . .

> ☆ "Please tell me more about what you and Joshua want to accomplish."
> ☆ "What are your strategic initiatives?"
> ☆ "What outcomes should be achieved?"

At this point, Dana probably shows zero ability to answer these polite queries or any other meaningful questions. Therefore, consider saying something like . . .

> "Dana, I could sure use your help. You and I both have an ethical responsibility to understand Joshua's goals and objectives. Let's take a peek at the calendar to find a convenient time for a telephone date, so the three of us can explore how we'll help Wonder Widgets. Other clients have found a brief call like this really is a simple and effective way to focus on results. How's your schedule and Joshua's on Wednesday or Thursday morning?"

Dana usually says something like, "Um, well, I really don't have to be part of the call. So why don't you just call Joshua Wednesday morning at eight o'clock?"

Key and powerful subtleties in this potential success script:

☆ Using "I could sure use your help . . ." or "I need your help . . ." is great language. (People love to help.)

☆ Using "ethical responsibility." (I really believe I have an ethical responsibility to visit with the company president. And Dana doesn't want to commit an ethical breach.)

Objection or obstacle:
"It would be cheaper for us to do this in-house."

Potential success script:
Consider . . .

> "It's easy to see why you'd feel that way. Other clients have initially considered an in-house solution, too—until they realized their learning curve would be significant, meaning the problem would continue to linger until they were up to speed . . . and that could take weeks or even months. Plus, their people would have to devote countless and sometimes frustrating

hours attempting to solve topics and issues they weren't experts in. This would lead to a drain on time, productivity, and revenue. What impact would these new pressures have on your people and profits?"

Also consider, some simple yet effective questions, like . . .

"How so?"
"What would your savings be?"
"How would you attain those savings?"

Questions and statements like the preceding help a decision maker quickly realize that an attempt "to save" really requires significant redirected resources of their time, energy, talent, and money. Ouch! Far better to use you!

Objection or obstacle:
"I'm still not sure if it'll work."

Potential success script:
Consider . . .

> "I understand your concern; you bring up an interesting point. Together, let's review how it'll work to meet and exceed your goals of . . ." (Refer to their specific objectives, needs, or desires.)
>
> "What else would you like to see or do so you're comfortable with its performance?"
>
> "How many satisfied customers would you like to chat with about how they eliminated the same problem of . . . or achieved . . .?"

Objection or obstacle:
"The price is still too high."

Potential success script:
Consider . . .

> "When you say 'too high,' could you please be more specific?"
>
> "Too high, meaning . . . ?"

"If your goal is to reduce the investment, which benefits would you like to eliminate?"

"If your goal is to do it for less, what value would you like to do without?"

Objection or obstacle:
"I'd like to think it over."

Potential success script:
Consider . . .

"That's really smart. This is an important decision. You *should* think it over. How much time do you need? Are you sure that's enough time?"

"Would it be fair to say, since you want to think this over, that you're giving this decision serious consideration?"

"Let's list the points you'd like to consider, so together we can address them to your total satisfaction." (Review Profit Point 28 on "Total satisfaction.")

"What will change, happen, or make a difference between now and then, that'll enable us to move forward?"

"So you're excited about the benefits and value of yadda, yadda, yadda. The only thing to resolve is . . . and you're confident we can do that by . . . ?"

"If we can eliminate that concern by solving it together now, would we then be able to (move to the next step, select a date for installation, etc.)?"

Objection or obstacle:
"You're too late. We bought one already."

Potential success script:
Consider . . .

"Excellent! How's it performing?"

"How has it helped you achieve your goals?"

"What areas, if any, have you been disappointed in? What impact has that had?"

"What would you do with an employee who wasn't performing?"

"How long do you want to struggle with something that's not delivering results?"

"Let's meet briefly to explore how to eliminate your frustration. How's your schedule on . . . ?"

Realize objections and obstacles are often simply delays and stalls. If they're not an official "no," they may really be a "not yet" waiting to become a "yes."

To get to the "yes" quickly, effectively, and profitably . . .

Go A.P.E.!

Anticipate.
Plan.
Execute.

Profit Point

31

Winning the inside fight.

People often tell me, "Jeff, some of my toughest battles aren't with customers; they're within my own company!"

They lament about how innovation is spurned or breakthroughs denied because they don't fit within one's rigid company culture or strict policies.

Their frustration is atypical or unusual, right? Because the folks at your company never attempt to kill great ideas or thwart possibilities.

Or do they?

If the following have ever been uttered in your hallowed halls, simply nod quietly, check appropriately, or scream wildly!

Here are 16 ways to kill a great idea or wallow in mediocrity:

1. That's not the way we do things here.
2. That'll never fly; it won't fit in with our culture.
3. That's against our policy.
4. We've never done it that way before.
5. We didn't invent it here, so we won't do it here.
6. We know that'll never work.
7. There's no budget.
8. We can't afford it.
9. We're just not ready to do that yet.

10. We're way too busy.

11. We'll be fine without it.

12. We shouldn't rock the boat.

13. Everything is fine; there's no need to upgrade or change.

14. We looked into that last year; no need to reconsider.

15. Our folks aren't properly trained.

16. There's no need to reinforce this message. Our people will take action on their own.

Now, if you're squirming in discomfort or writhing in pain, the next time you hear any of the preceding excuses, confidently reply with **three simple yet powerful words that generate breakthroughs, action, and results:**

Up until now!

P.I.T. Stop

P   Provocative or Playful

I   Inspirational or Informational

T   Thoughts or Theories

You Can Observe a Lot Just by Watching!

Spotted on a resume: "I enjoy participating in observing sports."
    Huh? Doesn't this mean this guy is a spectator?!

Flying Funnies

En route to Vail through Denver, my United Air Lines flight attendant or purser, D. J. Jaehnke, declared,

"We hope you have enjoyed giving us the business, because we sure have enjoyed . . . taking you for a ride!"

She then exclaimed,

"Before opening the overhead bins, please be careful, because as we all know . . . shift happens!"

Safety Signs

Spotted on I-17 North on the way to Sedona, Arizona:

Federal Prison: Do not stop for hitchhikers.

Pants Perplexity

I recently found in the pocket of a new pair of pants a slip of paper that declared:

"INSPETED BY #1."

Hmmm. It made me wonder—if #1 can't spell "inspected," how effective could he be at doing it?!

"Far more than our abilities, our choices show what we truly are."

> —*Professor Albus Dumbledore, headmaster,*
> *Hogwarts School of Witchcraft and Wizardry*

Profit Pillar

IV

A Profit Parade

32

Value on the vine!

There was once a farmer who had some beautiful yellow tomatoes, but couldn't sell them.

They were priced the same as the red tomatoes, but nobody wanted to buy yellow ones. He was stumped.

The yellow tomatoes were big, plump, and delicious. He even offered free slices on toothpicks. Folks gobbled them up, but still didn't buy.

Then the farmer was struck by creativity and the power of perception!

He put a sign next to the yellow tomatoes that read:

Gourmet! Organic! Low-Acid!

This was true. Yet it was true of any good tomato. The farmer also increased the price of the yellow tomatoes—by a dollar a pound.

By mid-morning, the yellows had sold out!

Profit Point

33

The innovative interview.

If you're looking for a new member of your sales team, do it with creativity, fun, and imagination. Any effective sales pro should be well prepared for the typical interview blather:

Tell me about yourself.

Why did you leave your last sales position?

What do you offer I can't find elsewhere?

What do you know about us?

Blah, blah, blah . . .

However, if you want to cut to the chase and find out quickly who can really think on their feet and communicate with articulate and insightful replies . . .

Try out these gems:

☆ Who are your heroes? How come?

☆ What book(s) are you currently reading?

☆ What's your philosophy of selling, service, or business?

☆ What are your values?

☆ What has been your biggest defeat or mistake? What did you learn from it? How did you bounce back?

☆ What would you do with this opportunity if you knew it was impossible to fail?

☆ What's your ideal work environment?

☆ What culture are you most successful in?

☆ What would your customers say they value most about you?

☆ What's your greatest strength?

☆ What professional area or skill would you like to improve on? How do expect to accomplish that?

☆ What are your hobbies and interests?

☆ What did your homework or research reveal about our company and our industry?

☆ What would you do if I asked you to lie for me? (By the way, if candidates are willing to lie or simply bend the truth for you, you don't want them! Escort them to the door or fire escape. Fast!)

Profit Point

34

Negotiation know-how!

Clients often ask me, "How can I become a better negotiator?"

That's an easy one. First, acknowledge that every negotiation is an evolutionary process. It changes with the introduction of a new objective or an unexpected decision maker.

Therefore, planned spontaneity or preparation combined with flexibility and creativity are crucial to your success.

**The following "dynamic dozen" are practical,
profit-producing, and ethical tips that'll immediately
help you maximize your success and results.**

1. **Negotiate** only with those who have the authority to make a decision.
2. **Anticipate and be prepared** to make value concessions, not compromises, and only if necessary.
3. **Know your objectives**, limits, and expectations, and don't compromise them.
4. **Know your customer's goals**, objectives, and expectations, and understand them.
5. **Identify the strengths** of you, your company, your product, or your service . . . and always communicate and reiterate them.

6. **Look at the big picture**, the long term . . . not the quick hit.

7. **When the judge rules in your favor**, get out of the court! Or said another way, when you get a favorable decision, say "thank you" and leave!

8. **The best time to get something** is when you give something.

9. **Be aware of deadlines** (real versus assumed).

10. **Know how to respond** to a totally unacceptable offer, either with a question, the twitch (which is physical or auditory disbelief), or silence.

11. **Be wary of** the decision maker who appears dumb or says little. It could be a ploy.

12. **Be willing to walk away** from a bad deal.

Profit Point

35

Houston, we have a problem!

I'm often asked, "Jeff, what do you think of the Enron fallout? And what can we learn?"

It pains me. It sticks in my craw. Fortunes lost. Lives destroyed.

As the facts and chaos continued to unravel, we were exposed to more acts of deception and deceit. Yet, thankfully, there was the courageous Sherron Watkins, who had the guts to blow her whistle and acknowledge, "Whoa, something stinks!"

In August of 2001, she wrote now dethroned Enron chairman Kenneth Lay a letter stating, "I am incredibly nervous that we will implode in a wave of accounting scandals."

If this was a Hollywood script, one might claim it was too farfetched. Yet as we discovered, this wasn't make-believe. It was a harsh reality.

And Enron's daily "reality script" was being written by fallen executives, devastated employees, and eager politicians, with help from lawyers, judges, accountants, regulators, legislators, and theoreticians.

And this Enron tale of tragedy became manna from heaven for B-school and law school profs. It featured greed, lies, and conflict—probably enough to fill a syllabus for the next decade!

As we soon realized, the key wasn't simply, "Who did what to whom and when?" Instead, it had to be, "What are the solutions and reforms for the future?"

John Dewey, an American philosopher and educator, developed a strategy for ethical decision making called *reflective morality*.

Dewey felt that upon reflection, thought, and deliberation, a decision maker could creatively imagine, rehearse, and evaluate several courses of action before reaching a conclusion. (Apparently the Enron execs weren't fans of Dewey!)

Adapting Dewey's framework, here are six steps to help you clarify responsibilities, eliminate misunderstandings, and conduct your sales career, business, and life with the highest possible ethical standards.

Step 1:
Identify the topic or issue causing your ethical dilemma.

Step 2:

List all of your possible choices.

Step 3:

List the possible consequences of each choice.

Step 4:

List the people affected by your choices.

Step 5:

Trade places. Put yourself in an empathetic position to understand how those just listed in Step 4 are affected by your choices. Bury your ego. Minimize your needs. Instead, maximize, for example, another's needs. How do your choices impact their lives, interests, and futures?

Step 6:

Make a decision. Then, take action! For without action, the dilemma not only lingers, it magnifies.

Ethical Standards of Excellence

To get an additional ethics perspective, I sought the help of Frank Bucaro. Frank helps organizations integrate ethical standards of excellence with solid business practices. He's also a gifted speaker and author (*Taking the High Road: How to Succeed Ethically When Others Bend the Rules*).

Frank is also a valued friend. Since 1986, we've had lots of fun discussions about life, ethics, and values.

Here are excerpts from a recent conversation with Frank:

Me: What lessons are to be learned from the Enron mess?

Frank Bucaro: Lesson 1: Just because a company has a code of ethics doesn't mean it uses it, believes it, or even models it.

It seems that Enron was saying it's appropriate for all except the high-level executives to live the code, but when it comes to "my" personal choices, ethics takes a backseat to profiteering.

Lesson 2: No decision affects only the one making it. Thousands of Enron workers lost their retirement savings due to the decisions of the few at the top.

Lesson 3: There must be accountability for decisions made. Someone or somebody must pay the price of cheating, stealing, profiting, or behaving in an unethical or illegal manner.

JB: What questions should one ask oneself if confronted by an ethical dilemma?

FB: Always consider what I call "the price to pay" for your decisions. If you cannot "pay the price," then walk away!

The decisions one makes in the hopes that no one finds out are usually wrong!

JB: What if you believe you are taking the high road, yet others still have a different perception?

FB: You have to live with yourself. We can't change other people. We can only influence them to want to change. We do this best by living out our values and ethics in a consistent manner.

If what is happening goes against your moral code, you have an obligation to choose the path and make the decision that helps you find peace within yourself.

JB: How does an organization create an ethical environment?

FB: It always starts at the top. Yet mere statements from on high do little for morale or successful implementation.

A code of ethics plus mission or values statements help, yet everybody must provide input to create ownership. Values are caught, not taught. Who you are says so much more than what you say.

Frank's perspective along with Dewey's steps should offer you a framework for future success.

So what's the best course of action for you? That's your decision. It's your future. Yet perhaps the best place to start is by asking yourself a simple question:

"Am I willing to lie, cheat, steal, bend the truth, or manipulate the facts? And if so, am I willing to explain my decision or action on the network news?"

Hmmm, that would have been an interesting question to pose in 2002 to suspended Olympic pair-skating judge Marie-Reine Le Gougne of France.

Profit Point

36

Hot town, summer in the city!

June 20, 2002:

It was going to be another scorcher in Houston. Tropical. And sticky.

As I glanced out the window of my hotel room, the hot morning sun was already glistening off the skyscrapers. One in particular caught my attention. The sun was bouncing off its reflective glass. This beautiful structure rose toward the sky, almost boasting of its supremacy.

This tall tower should have been a testament to truth, hard work, and the power of capitalism. Instead, it was a model of deceit. For it would forever be associated with creative accounting, cooked books, and boardroom betrayal.

I shook my head in disappointment, yet acknowledged the irony of my morning. For in just a few hours, I would be delivering a keynote address to a corporate client's accounting team. The focus: ethics and values.

My client and their people get it. They know the significance of integrity, even if it hurts the bottom line.

Yet there, staring down at me, with its external majesty and internal mayhem, was the Enron building.

Enron, your classic corporate miscreant!

Fifteen minutes later, there was a knock at the door. It was room service. Oscar entered and set my breakfast on the desk. He then stared out the window and declared, "Enron. Some bad people who did bad things."

Simple yet powerful words.

Blow the Whistle

The Enron meltdown was thankfully brought to our societal microscope in August 2001, when Sherron Watkins had the guts to blow the whistle.

Yet I often wondered: Why did she do it?

I was able to answer that question with the help of her lawyer. To most of the world he's Philip Hilder, attorney-at-law. To me he's simply Phil, a valued friend.

Phil and I have known each other for more than 20 years. His best buddy, Steve Krafft, is a close friend of mine. (Steve and I were radio partners here in Chicago from 1982 to 1985.)

On the evening of June 19, 2002, Phil and I got together in the lobby of the downtown Houston Hyatt to once again catch up on family, friends, and the Enron debacle.

When I asked Phil to tell me about Sherron Watkins, here's what he said:

☆ She was raised to do the right thing.

☆ She had good role models; her parents were teachers.

☆ She still works at Enron, where on the executive floors she's considered an outcast or pariah.

☆ Her decisions have been influenced by a strong moral code of conduct.

☆ Her choices were about values, not merely numbers.

And according to Phil, here are some lessons to be learned:

☆ Have the courage to challenge authority.

☆ Do not blindly follow leaders without asking tough questions.

☆ Control your own destiny.

☆ Do not allow your financial fate to be tied to only your company.

☆ Let values guide your decisions.

Integrity is based on truth. Oscar Wilde said, "Truth is never pure, and rarely simple." Truth may not be simple, but the complexities of deceit and situational ethics are monumental.

 The greatest advantage of honesty is that it doesn't require a good memory!

Your *word* represents your credibility, reputation, and character. Integrity is nonnegotiable. Its impact is powerful. It's good character, goodwill, and good sense. Buyers might expect you to sit at the bargaining table with a sharpened pencil, a laptop computer, and savvy negotiation strategy. But there should be no need for a lie detector, belief barometer, or ethics evaluator.

As an ethical sales pro, you may be perceived as unique. And it's a valuable, respected, and appreciated "unique." Just like a diamond is worth more when it's unique and rare, so are you. You possess a special power, an aura of influence. Your prospects and customers believe in you. They like you. They trust you. And they buy from you—again and again.

Profit Point

37

Peddler or partner?

Don't be driven by only commissions, quotas, or contests. These are *your* motivators, not your decision maker's.

Don't peddle products and services.

Instead, deliver results and value.

Today's buyers don't simply want a product or a service, they want *you*.

And they expect you to be a consultant. A strategic adviser. A partner.

Partners are invaluable. Vendors are expendable.

Profit Point

38

Driving the C-class.

Are all decision makers created equal? Well, yes and no.

While every decision maker may have the ability to say "yes," it's not necessarily their "yes" you want.

Some prospects or customers might only be able to say "yes":

- ☆ To certain decisions.
- ☆ To decisions up to a specific dollar amount.
- ☆ To decisions that protect or preserve their little world, territory, or fiefdom.
- ☆ To decisions that will make them look good.
- ☆ To decisions that will protect their butt.
- ☆ To decisions with little risk.
- ☆ To decisions that are limited in scope and impact.

Are the preceding decision makers valuable? Sure. But not if they're obstacles to helping your clients, customers, and prospects grow and prosper.

A client once declared, "You have to discover who is a pretender and who is a player."

Therefore, if you want to maximize results with "players"—you need to, as another client likes to say, "Play in a different sandbox!"

This sandbox has finer sand. Cooler pails. And better shovels. It's the "arena" or "toy territory" of the C-class decision maker.

The C-class decision maker is likely to be a:

☆ Chairman   ☆ Director

☆ CEO   ☆ CFO

☆ Owner   ☆ COO

☆ President   ☆ Executive vice president

☆ Partner   ☆ Senior vice president

☆ Principal   ☆ Vice president

Could there be other C-class titles? Of course. I've worked with lots of C-class decision makers with other titles. But a title is secondary to a C-class decision maker's decision-making clout and style. Cs share common characteristics.

C-class decision makers are all focused on:

☆ **Output.**

☆ **Outcomes.**

☆ **Results.**

☆ **Improved conditions.**

Plus, they have the ability and authority to give a thumbs-up to significant investments. They look at ROI or return on investment, not ATS or amount of time spent! They don't watch the clock; they watch the results.

CEOs and C-class decision makers say things to me like:

☆ "Jeff, get it done!"

☆ "Make it happen!"

☆ "Drive the process!"

☆ "Report the results!"

High-level decision makers especially respect honesty. Because all too often, they don't get the real story from their ranks. That's why they value and are willing to invest in an outside perspective—mine. I'm apolitical. I have no bias, predisposition, or personal agenda to advance.

World's Shortest Job Interview

Over the years, lots of CEOs and presidents have made me the offer they thought I couldn't refuse: "Jeff, come work for us!"

My response: "I'd be a lousy employee because you might lose what you value most, my candor and fresh eyes." Though disappointed, they all agree.

My focus is always on what's in their best interest, even if it means sharing tough-to-hear insights or suggestions.

A CEO of a multibillion-dollar company once declared,

"Jeff, what I like about you is you never protect your butt and you never kiss mine!"

I assure this by asking C-class decision makers a simple, yet powerful question. (We first covered this question in Profit Pillar II.)

"As I discover facts and insights about your people, culture, and organization, would you prefer that when I share them with you, I'm honest or diplomatic?"

The answer is always the same. Although it might be accompanied by a slight squirm, a minor grimace, and a penetrating bite of the lower lip, all my C-class clients declare:

"I want it honest!"

"Give it to me straight!"

"Hit me right between the eyes."

"Make it the truth, even if it hurts."

While a C-class decision maker might not want to hear what I have to tell him or her, each always realizes that early in our relationship they gave me permission to be honest. And *that* always works to their advantage.

Once, a CEO asked me to observe and assess his contribution to one of his organization's cultural initiatives—a speech to his troops. Before he sought my opinion and analysis, he turned to other members of his team and asked, "So on a scale of 1 to 10, how'd I do?"

They enthusiastically exclaimed:

"Never better. A 10!"

"Powerful! Captivating! A 9!"

"They loved you. Another 9!"

"Wouldn't change a thing. Make it a 10!"

I sat silent. Expressionless.

And then he turned, stared, and asked, "Well, Jeff, what do *you* think?"

I calmly said, "Do you want me to be honest or diplomatic?"

His team flashed looks of disbelief. Eyes bulged. Jaws dropped. Though no words were spoken, you knew what they were thinking: "Blackman is nuts." "This guy is crazy." "Oh, no, our CEO is going to rip Blackman apart."

The CEO glanced back, smiled, and said, "As always, Jeff, be honest!"

I replied, "There's good news and there's great news. First, the good news. You're at a 6." (While there was an almost audible gasp from the team, the CEO listened intently.) I continued, "And the great news is, you'll soon be at a 10. Here's a list of eight things to consider." (As I gave the CEO specific upgrades and action steps, he feverishly took notes and nodded his head in agreement.) When I was done, he looked up from his legal pad and said, "That's great stuff, Jeff. This really helps."

After years of working with top-level executives and senior leaders, I've discovered:

> **Big decisions for big bucks . . .**
>
> **are made by big people . . .**
>
> **who live in a big world . . .**
>
> **who want to generate . . .**
>
> **big results.**

Therefore, if you want to play at the top, you have to understand those who are at the top. So here's a list of 35 "C-class commonalities."

C-class decision makers:

1. Have big egos (that's healthy).

2. Are driven by results.

3. Love to talk about their vision or plan for the future.

4. Will always discuss strategies that increase sales, revenues, shareholder value, volume, average sale, or market share.

5. Will always discuss strategies that protect, preserve, or grow their company.

6. Make things happen; they take action.

7. Are decisive, to the point, and direct.

8. Are pressed for time; they often run late.

9. Like quick overviews, the 30,000-foot view, simple summations, bullet points, and short messages with lots of meat (i.e., voice mail, e-mail, print).

10. Love to talk about themselves, yet even more about their people and their results.

11. Love to talk about what's on their plate, their Focus Five, their strategic initiatives, and their quarterly goals.

12. Value candor and honesty.

13. Detest know-it-alls, poor preparation, nonresponsive answers, b.s.

14. Don't like surprises.

15. Value choice (i.e., alternative value strategies or results strategies).

16. Make the details easy when they want to work with you.

17. Are easily accessible when they value their relationship with you.

18. Don't get hung up on fine print; they focus on relationships and results.

19. Value loyalty, commitment, and passion.

20. Seek outside counsel, guidance, and advice.

21. Value innovation, creativity, and unique solutions.

22. Love a challenge and are not risk-averse.

23. Like the limelight, recognition, and acknowledgment of their success.

24. Want metrics to measure results.

25. Expect you to be punctual and to honor your deliverables or deadlines.

26. Expect a high level of trust, respect, and confidentiality.

27. Can be demanding, yet are loyal to those who deliver.

28. Focus on value and results, not products and price.

29. Reward success.

30. Value collaborative relationships.

31. Value partners not vendors (vendors are expendable, while partners are invaluable).

32. Value intelligence and polite persistence.

33. Demand and expect accountability.

34. Live in a value-driven world versus a time-driven world, meaning they value output, not input, for time merely shows hours devoted or energy expended and "Cs" are focused on outcomes and results.

35. Approve or help others approve BIG agreements for BIG bucks that they expect to generate BIG value and BIG results.

When you design your sales and marketing efforts and commit your focus to numbers 1 through 34, then number 35 becomes easy!

Profit Point

39

Pitcher perfect.

For the past few years, Curt Schilling, an Arizona Diamondbacks pitcher, has been one of the top hurlers in major league baseball. During the 2001 season, Schilling and his teammate, Randy Johnson, led the Diamondbacks to stunning victories and a remarkable seven-game World Series championship against the favored New York Yankees. (That year, Schilling and Johnson were also corecipients of the World Series most valuable player award.)

Schilling is obviously successful on the field. Yet a major reason for his success, is what he does off the field—especially with his pregame preparation and planning.

Most pitchers study hitters: their likes, dislikes, pitch preferences, location habits, or tendencies to swing or not swing on certain ball and strike counts. Schilling does all of this. However, he has also upgraded his homework assignments to include studying umpires—methodically and analytically.

Schilling once said,

"I keep a book on umpires. When I go into a series, I know who my umpire is going to be, so I have an idea what the strike zone is going to be like."

He went on to say,

"It's command. Control is the ability to throw strikes. In the big leagues, everybody has control. Command is the ability to throw quality strikes. And when you add preparation to command, good things will happen."

It's also interesting to note that Schilling earned $6,500,000 during the 2001 season. Following his stellar performance that year, he got a hefty raise. His salary for the 2002 season was $10,000,000. With results come rewards!

How prepared are you?

For example:

What questions do you have ready to go for a meeting with a prospect or a customer?

What potential obstacles are you anticipating?

What responses have you prepared to overcome those obstacles?

Who are your likely competitors?

What might they offer that you don't? Is it a true apples to apples comparison?

Planning turns promise into potential.
Preparation turns performance into profitability.
Here are three of my favorites quotes about preparation and planning:

"Planning is bringing the future into the present so that you can do something about it now."

—*Alan Lakein*

"Thoroughness characterizes all successful people. Genius is the art of taking infinite pains. All great achievement has been characterized by extreme care, infinite painstaking, even to the minutest detail."

—*Elbert Hubbard*

"Meticulous planning will enable everything one does to appear spontaneous."

—*Mark Caine*

Remember, to win, you must plan and prepare to win!

Profit Point

40

Get CRE8IV!

A workshop participant recently said to me,

> "Jeff, we are living in the days of the Jetsons, but we are serving our customers like the days of the Flintstones."

There's always a better way. Your challenge is to find it.

Here are nine creative strategies designed to boost your brain, to crank your cranium, to turn creativity into cash, and to convert possibilities into profit.

1. Be on the prowl.
2. Stare with your ears, listen with your eyes.

3. Keep it.
4. Incubate.
5. Seek outside counsel.
6. Get abstract.
7. Trust your gut.
8. Water it and watch it grow.
9. Do something.

Be on the Prowl . . .

Read. Then read some more—especially outside your area of expertise or traditional areas of interest. Head to a bookstore or newsstand and buy a book or magazine, where you might exclaim, "I can't believe I'm buying this!" Or hop online and surf the Web. Ride the wave of wonder. Give yourself permission to bust beyond your perceived boundaries. Seek fresh content. Open your eyes to new stuff. Play with the possibilities.

About a year ago, as part of a project for a new series of books, I was stumped. My creative inspiration for an impactful logo was frozen in futility. When my graphic designer kept asking, "What do you envision?" I'd reply, "Ain't sure. Still thinking. Still looking."

And then, one memorable night, I received the lightning bolt of inspiration I was waiting for. Where did it come from? One of my kids' magazines. With the turn of a page, boom, there it was! A publication geared to 11- and 12-year-olds stirred my creative juices. (Okay, so maybe I think and act like their target audience, but that's a discussion for another book or therapy session!)

Stare with Your Ears,
Listen with Your Eyes . . .

While focus is crucial, be sure to still look in all directions. Pay attention to the world around you. There's lots of cool stuff happening! Look at billboards and signs. Walk into stores you've never visited before. Politely eavesdrop on conversations. Take a different route from point A to B. Then wonder, "Whoa, when did they build that?! Where did that come from?" See new things.

When you're at an airport, a mall, or a restaurant, activate all your senses. Look. Listen. Smell. Be ready and receptive to discover and uncover the possibilities. Because sometimes they sneak up on you. The inspiration for my *Carpe A.M., Carpe P.M.—Seize Your Destiny* book title came from a passing bus billboard promoting a discotheque in Florida.

Keep It . . .

When an idea hits you, capture it. *Now!* Don't lose it. Mumble into a recorder. Send yourself an e-mail. Leave yourself a voice mail. Write it down. (I keep paper and pencil in my car, next to my bed, in the bathroom, near the treadmill, etc.)

Start a file (either hard copy or electronic) for your ideas, then categorize them (i.e., new products, new services, new clients, new strategies, etc.).

Incubate . . .

The idea hits you; cool! You wrote it down; excellent! Now, forget about it—for an hour or a day. Get a good night's rest. Sleep on it. Let your subconscious kick in.

Time is a miraculous contributor to upgrades and improvements. It brings clarity. Use time to your advantage.

Seek Outside Counsel . . .

Ask others for their input. Capitalize on multiple brainpower. Remember, "Where all think alike, no one thinks very much." Or, to state it another way, "When two people are always in agreement, one of them ain't necessary."

Get Abstract . . .

Let the bizarre, absurd, or goofy creep into your thought process. Defy the rules of conformity. I've always believed if enough people tell you you're nuts, you're probably headed in the right direction!

Trust Your Gut . . .

That strange, quirky sensation that stirs in your tummy is usually right. Listen to it. Trust your instincts. Don't let your intuition lose to the cynics or voices of logical debate and doubt.

Water It and Watch It Grow . . .

Crank the H_2O. Something miraculous happens near water. When I'm in the shower or shaving, my subconscious creativity is in turbodrive. Let your mind wander. Often, the journey to greatness doesn't take a straight or linear path. Let water unleash your creative spirit.

> *"Everyone who has taken a shower has an idea. It's the person who gets out of the shower, dries off, and does something about it who makes a difference."*
>
> —*Nolan Bushnell, entrepreneur*
> *(founder: Atari and Chuck E. Cheese)*

Do Something . . .

Take action. Turn ideas into implementation, and inspiration into execution. There's a big difference between thinking and doing! As Ben Franklin once stated,

"Well done is better than well said."

Profit Point

41

Lost or found?

A subscriber to my free e-zine, *The Results Report*, posed an interesting question:

"Jeff, I recently lost a client. What did I do wrong?"

I replied:

To give you a deeper insight and more on-target explanation, I need to know more details. However, there's a pretty good likelihood you blew it in one or more ways.

So take a deep gulp. Be brutally honest. Review the following. And then you'll know better than anyone else where you goofed.

You may have lost a client if . . .

1. You promised a lot, but underdelivered.
2. You or your people were rude, uncaring, or indifferent.
3. You stopped listening because you knew all the answers.
4. You remembered the importance of customer acquisition, but you forgot about the significance of satisfaction and retention.

5. You forgot that individuals make decisions and you began to take for granted or ignored the value in your relationships.

6. Your product or service has declining value or quality.

7. You stopped communicating in a timely and effective manner.

8. Your client's needs and expectations changed, but your strategies and solutions didn't.

9. You committed an ethical breach.

10. You began to think you were selling a commodity with no differential competitive advantage except a lower price.

11. You missed deadlines and deliverables.

12. Your customer found somebody else who wasn't doing 1 through 11.

Are you in jeopardy of losing a customer? If so, the time to take corrective action, is *now*!

By the way, a "lost" customer or client may be only temporarily "misplaced." Where they are really depends on where you are.

Go find them!

(To receive *The Results Report*, simply go to www.jeffblackman.com.)

P.I.T. Stop

P Provocative or Playful

I Inspirational or Informational

T Thoughts or Theories

Doggie Dollars

My nephew Josh is an entrepreneur. When he was eight years old, he became the CEO and founder of Backyard Wipe Out. Here's an excerpt from the flyer he printed and distributed throughout his neighborhood:

Wednesday is Wipe Out Day. That is when I will clean your dog's poop. A 15-pound or less dog is 50 cents. A 16-pound or more dog is 75 cents. Two or more dogs are $1.00. There is a 25-cent surcharge to haul the poop away or you may keep it for your trash.

Josh's entrepreneurial spirit reinforces the axiom that one person's _____ is another person's fortune!

Tram Trouble

On the airport tram in Las Vegas:

Stranger: So did you win?

Me: You bet! How about you?

Stranger: Nope. Big loser. Lost my money. And, lost my girl-friend.

Me: Sorry. Which disappoints you the most?

Stranger: The money!

If you aren't going all the way, why go at all?

Profit Pillar

V

Communicate
& Conquer

42

Why? 'CAUS!

On a daily basis, I confront the world's toughest negotiators. No, not clients. My kids! They're relentless. They're aggressive. And they don't know the meaning of the word "no!" To them, "no" simply sets the stage for dialogue.

Therefore, I've learned a powerful response to their constant queries of "Why?" For now when they ask, "Why?"—I'm conditioned to exclaim, "Because!"

It's simple. Direct. And a momentary stopgap.

However, "because" is two syllables and it takes too long to repeatedly utter. Therefore, with extensive training, I've developed the ability to now answer the frequent "Why?" questions with only one syllable, "'Caus." (Pronounced: *cuz*.)

They ask, "Why?" I declare, "'Caus!"

And I realized, wouldn't this be a wonderful retort to a prospect who wonders, "Why should we use you?" And all you need to confidently respond with is "'Caus!"

Here's what I mean.

What if "'Caus" stood for:

Constant

Awesome

Unduplicatable

Supremacy

And that's exactly what *you* deliver!
    'CAUS meaning:

Constant: ongoing, all-the-time, nonstop.

Awesome: phenomenal, incredible, extraordinary.

Unduplicatable: can't be copied, unique, one-of-a-kind.

Supremacy: highest quality, superiority, the ultimate.

When you offer the marketplace constant, awesome, unduplicatable supremacy, your customers benefit. They tell the world. And you profit!

Here's a simple example of 'CAUS in action. As you may know, here in Chicago the hot dog is considered haute cuisine! And one of the best places to devour this Chicago tradition is at the Superdawg Drive-In.

Superdawg is literally a nostalgic throwback to the 1950s. Carhops attach a tray to your car window that's stacked high with "snap when you bite 'em" Superdawgs, hot and crispy Superfries, and thick and rich Supershakes.

And the Superdawg receipt boldly declares:

"Our family has been thrilling customers with superfood and friendly service since 1948!"

Wow! How's that for a 'CAUS declaration!?

My wife and I even stopped for a Superdawg one night after a wedding. The parking lot was full, but we were the only ones in a formal gown and a tuxedo. (I was in the tux!)

So how can you create constant, awesome, unduplicatable supremacy with:

☆ Your products
☆ Your services
☆ Your promotional literature

☆ Your delivery
☆ Your web site
☆ Your phone contact

☆ Your image or "brand" ☆ Your packaging
☆ Your correspondence ☆ Your merchandising
☆ Your telephone reception/greeting ☆ Your relationships

And most important, with . . .

You!

Oh, when you're in Chicago and would like to witness and taste "constant, awesome, unduplicatable supremacy" at Superdawg, call me. Lunch is my treat!

Profit Point

43

First impressions.

Two of my clients, Nancy Katz and Loyd Hanson from Principal Residential Mortgage, told me a great story about one of their customers, Stanley Kirst and his team at Platinum Capital.

Stanley and his team really know the importance of first impressions.

Their five receptionists all answer the phone with:

**"It's a great day at Platinum Capital. This is (name),
your Director of First Impressions. How may I help you?"**

Whoa! What a winner!
Sure beats the following, which I've heard:

☆ "Law offices."
☆ "Yes."
☆ "Three-four-two-four."
☆ "Hello."

How come so many companies allow a receptionist who is poorly trained, unenthusiastic, and disinterested to be their "voice to the world"? Is this person likely to be a "positive PR agent" or an "ambassador of goodwill"? Unlikely. Instead, their more appropriate title might be "Director of Lost, Blown, and Disappearing Opportunities."

When I recently called a client's distribution facility to interview one of their inside salespeople in preparation for an upcoming program, I was abruptly placed on hold—for four minutes and seven seconds. Absurd!

To me, this was valuable research (which I shared with the president, so immediate changes could be made). But a customer or a prospect might have simply hung up. And this seemingly minor indiscretion could jeopardize a positive and profitable relationship forever. The problem is, you may never know!

Prospects or disgruntled customers simply find another individual or company who *will* pay attention to them. They seldom give you a polite buzz back stating, "Sorry we couldn't chat. You made a lousy first impression, so I signed a big deal with your competitor!"

Another client, EPT, is an extremely successful apartment management company with multiple communities throughout the United States, Mexico, and Europe. When you call one of their properties, you might hear a leasing specialist or manager exclaim:

"It's your lucky day . . ." or

"It's all about you . . ."

This upbeat and warm hospitality is even evident at EPT's corporate headquarters in El Paso, Texas. When I call, the phone is usually answered by Paula Eaton. Paula is always a dynamic and friendly combination of enthusiasm, goodwill, and optimism.

Recently, I told Paula, "You always have such a positive attitude." She responded, "Jeff, it's important to you. It's important to me. And it's more important that you take it home with you."

Russ Vandenburg, EPT's president and CEO, reiterated to me during a conversation how valuable Paula is to the EPT team.

By the way, EPT stands for: excellence, pride, and teamwork. And that's evident with every phone call.

So what impression are you, your receptionist(s), and your company conveying with incoming phone calls? If it isn't positive, it's losing you customers. It's costing you money! Whatta ya going to do about it?

Here's one more cool thing the folks at Platinum Capital do. When you visit their office in Irvine, California, a "Director of First Impressions" announces over the intercom:

"Attention, Platinum, (your name) is visiting us."

The announcement is followed by a big cheer from the Platinum team!

Heck, wouldn't you want to do business with folks who provide thunderous applause at your presence?! And think of the upgrade possibilities; 10,000-watt spotlights, marching bands, and frenzied paparazzi!

Profit Point

44

Psychiatric help!

Yeah, it worked!

Your sales or marketing message—whether it's an ad, a direct mail piece, a well-timed phone call, or any other creative sales or marketing tool—creates enough interest to convert a suspect into a prospect.

They say, "Let's meet!" Phew. Step one is successful!

You meet. The chemistry is cooking. You bond. They love you, and assure you a decision is on its way. Cool! Looks like you're victorious in step two.

And now, you wait. Paint is drying. And wait. Grass is growing. And wait. Nada. Bupkus. Zip. Nuthin' is happenin'. Sound familiar? Ouch!

Clients often share with me their similar frustrations when their prospects don't return their phone calls or respond to their e-mails, faxes, and letters. They are forever stuck in prospect purgatory, the maddening and inhospitable land of no decision.

So when they request my counsel to combat this dilemma, I'll often suggest they call their "psychiatrist."

Huh?

Well, first I should mention I've been very fortunate. It's unusual for a prospect not to respond to my voice mails or e-mails. (That's likely because I'm dealing with prospects who are referrals, or they found me via an article, book, or speaking engagement. I don't attempt to woo frigid prospects in cold calls.)

However, on that rare occasion when my polite and persistent attempts to yak with a prospect are unsuccessful, I seek medical help!

My theory is if traditional attempts at communication aren't working, it's okay to go crazy!

The following is verbatim language I've used with prospects who are still suspects:

HELP!

I haven't slept in days!

Am going without food and water!

Am waiting near the phone!

Am hovering over the fax machine!

Am checking e-mails every 10 minutes!

Yet my clients whom you wanted to contact and I still haven't heard from you.

My psychiatrist said, "Stop worrying!" He said you'll contact all of us soon about how I can help you and your team like we continue to help others maximize results and profitability.

Like the CEO who e-mailed me . . .

[Will feature excerpts from the e-mail.]

Or the president and vice president who wrote . . .

[Will feature excerpts from the letter(s).]

We're all waiting to hear from you!

Please let me know what our game plan is before I lose even more sleep and weight!

Okay, is the preceding crazy? Maybe. But it works.

Folks will then call or e-mail me and apologize for the delay. (They even thank me for getting their attention in a fun and unique way. They'll also say they want to be sure I'm eating and sleeping again!)

The purpose of this "loony language" is simple: to generate . . .

☆ Interest.
☆ Dialogue.
☆ Opportunity.
☆ Results.
☆ Outcomes.
☆ Satisfied clients.

**Remember, when the norm, standard, or status quo
ain't producing the results you want, go nuts!
Do the unexpected! Bust out of the box!**

It works. Big time!

Profit Point

45

On the way to this, I found that!

Recently, I suggested to a financial services client that their advisers use Internet search engines to discover what others in their industry are doing and saying to promote their products, services, and solutions.

For example, I recommended they consider doing searches for:

☆ Fee-based planners.

☆ Investment advisers.

☆ Financial advisers.

☆ Fee-only planners.

☆ Financial planners.

How come? Because they, like you, can quickly use the Web as a direct and indirect source of inspiration—for language, concepts, and phraseology.

Often, when you search for stuff that's merely related to your business, you can discover some powerful possibilities.

Here's a similar strategy. I constantly scour magazines and articles for captivating communication I can easily adapt for potential use.

The following examples may have direct application to you and your business. They can influence how you communicate in print, as well as,during client meetings or prospect conversations.

From the March 18, 2002, issue of *BusinessWeek*:

Excerpt from a Duke Energy Ad

"We didn't become a leader by wearing blinders. We see the subtleties. The opportunities overlooked by others. It is this intimacy with detail, and the ability to step back and see beyond, which give us perspective."

How can you adapt the preceding? Imagine that a prospect asks, "So what makes you so special?"

You might answer, "Extremely satisfied clients like (name drop) tell us we're focused on the details and the subtleties of their business. They feel this ability gives us and them a unique perspective to capitalize on opportunities that might be overlooked or missed by others."

Excerpt from a Novartis Ad for a Drug Therapy for Eyesight Deterioration

". . . an innovative force that's bringing new optimism and hope . . . think what's possible."

You might stress, "Clients like (name drop) tell us we're an innovative partner and creative force, helping them achieve new results and possibilities. Like the time we (refer to case studies, metrics, goals met and exceeded, statistics, testimonials, etc.)."

Excerpt from an Ad for Lufthansa

"Wherever you want to go, we make it easier for you to get there."

You could emphasize, "Our clients like (name drop) especially value the easy or hassle-free way we . . ."

As you can tell, the possibilities are huge. So be willing to take the direct, indirect, and side roads to results!

Profit Point

46

E-savvy versus Eeeh sorry!

Are you spending more time online, especially corresponding via e-mail with clients, prospects, and your team? Thought so.

Here are some guidelines to follow, so you'll be e-savvy versus eeeh sorry!

These 15 simple, yet impactful strategies will make your e-mails both meaningful and memorable:

1. Be conversational in tone.
2. If you don't want others to see it, don't send it. (Remember, it's called the World Wide Web for a reason. One click can quickly cause chaos!)
3. Create specific and/or creative subject lines, but nothing that causes confusion or misinterpretation or makes your message appear to be spam.
4. Never be angry, accusatory, or sarcastic.
5. Use short sentences, write in paragraphs, and avoid using all-uppercase words (they seem to YELL at you. Use them only for EMPHASIS.)
6. Proofread, knock out typos and bad grammar.
7. Write it, read it, and then ask yourself: "Can I make it better?" and, "Is there anything that might be misunderstood?"

8. Consider referencing the sender's specific language. For example, place between arrows . . .

   >>their question, comment, etc.<<

   and then give your response.

9. Have a unique parting salutation—for example, my use of "Creatively yours."

10. Use a signature block with your name, title, contact info, web site, favorite quote, an assistant's contact info, or a Web link.

11. Cc others who are part of the decision-making process.

12. Keep easy-access desktop files of template language, as well as key correspondence received and sent.

13. Be patient; use time to your advantage (while e-mail affords the luxury of instantaneous replies, that immediacy may eliminate the benefits of reflection and deliberation). Being speedy is not the same as being smart.

14. Avoid attached files (unless they're necessary and expected). Attachments require the recipient to do one more thing, plus there's the ever-present fear of the dreaded virus.

15. When appropriate, include a call to action (either you or the recipient will do something). For example, set a date for a meeting, reach agreement on an issue or question, make a decision, promise to send something, or honor a deadline or deliverable.

Profit Point

47

Toot your horn!

Your prospects might often ask, "Why should we pick you?" Here's how you can respond without sounding pompous or boastful.

An effective way to translate value to a prospect or referred lead is with testimonial endorsements. Your clients are probably willing to say lots of nice things about you. Yet perhaps you haven't asked them.

It's important to stress that the only way to secure favorable comments is by first doing your job: to meet clients' expectations and to exceed them!

Whether clients say incredible things about you in print, via e-mail, or on the phone, your real challenge is in using these words of praise to your advantage.

The next time a prospect asks:

"Why should we use you?"

"What makes you so special?"

"What will you do for us that others can't?"

Here's my suggestion. Don't answer. That's right, don't answer. At least not from your perspective.

If you begin to tell a prospect what makes you so special, from whose viewpoint are you answering? Yours! And you're biased. Even if it's the truth.

Shift into a third-party testimonial strategy.

Say something like,

"That's a great question and a fair one to ask. It's also a tough one for me to answer, because I guess I'm somewhat biased. Instead, let me share with you what three other clients said about our working relationship and results."

Here, you can:

☆ Fax them letters.
☆ Repeat statements told to you.
☆ Read from thank-you notes.
☆ Send copies of e-mails.
☆ Play audio or video testimonials.

Testimonials offer tremendous power and credibility.

They're especially valuable if your prospect knows the testimonial endorser. I actually had one decision maker exclaim, "Ernie said that about you? He doesn't like anybody—you must really be good!" This fellow quickly went from being a suspect—to a prospect—to a client!

The third-party testimonial strategy helps you toot your own horn, with some assistance. While you hold the horn, your testimonial endorsers play the notes!

Profit Point

48

Image impact.

Do first impressions matter? Only if you want to have the opportunity to make a second impression!

It isn't fair, but it's fact: First impressions influence buying decisions. And especially when buyers can't physically hold or see your product or service, they try to find reassurance. That reassurance or peace of mind is often provided by your presence and professionalism.

Roz Usheroff, author of *Customize Your Career: How to Develop Winning Strategies to Move Up, Move Ahead, or Move On* and a client who teaches others the "Art of Wow," says,

"Professionalism is the intangible quality that stamps your presence in the business world with integrity and purpose.
It encompasses your communication style, level of expertise, and interpersonal skills."

Daily, decision makers are bombarded by countless external stimuli: from travel, work, advertising, the media, and your competitors. Many times, these external factors and buying influencers are analyzed quickly. Buyers make snap judgments and then are off and running, ready to attack the next crisis. Therefore, you want to make sure every judgment made about your products, services, company, communication, and especially *you* is positive and favorable.

According to a friend of mine, communications specialist Lynn Pearl, "You have only five seconds when you enter a room to make a positive impression. A confident manner characterized by a strong stride, a friendly smile, good posture, and a genuine sense of energy commands respect." Studies have even shown a firm handshake, good eye contact, and simply remembering names are critical sales skills.

How well do you begin or cement a relationship within the first few minutes of meeting someone?

The following questions were designed to help you find the answer. Please respond to these questions with "always," "occasionally," or "rarely" as they apply to you and your business situation, sales environment, or style.

1. **When you approach a prospect/client/customer, do you convey confidence?**

   Always   Occasionally   Rarely

2. **Do you offer to shake hands first—and is your handshake firm and strong?**

   Always   Occasionally   Rarely

3. **Do you repeat someone's name and make sure you're pronouncing it properly?**

   Always   Occasionally   Rarely

4. **Do you greet people with a smile in person and on the phone?**

   Always   Occasionally   Rarely

5. **Do you focus on your prospect or client?**

   Always   Occasionally   Rarely

6. **Do you listen effectively?**

   Always   Occasionally   Rarely

7. **To show you were listening, do you *recap* the individual's key points and ask appropriate follow-up questions?**

   Always   Occasionally   Rarely

8. **Do you avoid interrupting others?**

   Always   Occasionally   Rarely

9. **Do your words, expressions, and body language convey a positive attitude?**

   Always   Occasionally   Rarely

10. **When you make a *promise* to do something, do you do it?**

    Always   Occasionally   Rarely

So how's your image impact?

Profit Point

49

The Rule of 4:1

Are your sales and business-development letters, client correspondence, or promotional materials too ego-driven?

If you're like most folks or companies, the answer is an unequivocal and unfortunate "Yes!"

Now I'm a big fan of a big ego, but not when it gets in the way of results.

Here's a simple test:

Take a scrutinizing look at *your stuff* (i.e., brochures, letters, etc.) with a red pen. Every time you use your company's name or the words:

☆ *I.*

☆ *Me.*

☆ My.

☆ *Mine.*

circle it.

Every time you use your client's or prospect's name or company or the words:

☆ *You.*

☆ *Your.*

underline it.

Now, count them up. How many circles? How many underlines?

If your "you" type words don't outnumber your "I" type words by at least 4:1, you're spending way too much time focused on the wrong person.

As you know, folks are more interested in *their* story than your story. Don't tell them how great you are. Instead, tell them how great you'll make them! Develop and maintain a "you" focus versus an "I" focus.

This subtle change in your writing style will have a dramatic impact on the tone, attitude, and impact of your words and results. (By the way, the principles of the Rule of 4:1 also apply to oral communication.)

Here's more proof. When you look at a long list of names, whose name do you find first? Of course, yours. When you look at a picture with lots of people, whose face do you search for first? Of course, yours.

It's always more visually appealing to your readers/viewers to see stuff that highlights them. Their eye naturally gravitates to their self-interest. It's not selfish. It's just factual. It's human nature. And that's okay.

The key is to know it. And capitalize on it. This message was reinforced in an unlikely setting.

Mirror, Mirror on the Wall

Every three to four weeks, I see Vicki Jones for her expertise. Vicki is one smart woman. She's not a consultant, but ought to be. She's not a therapist, but could be. Instead, Vicki is an extremely busy and successful hair stylist.

And a primary reason for her success is her focus on and commitment to her customers. For example, at Vicki's station, her mirror is not adorned with or cluttered by pictures of her family and pets, or notes reminding her to pick up a gallon of milk.

Instead, the only thing you see on/in Vicki's mirror is your reflection. Vicki told me this was a strategic decision. She said, "The highlight and focus must always be on the customer sitting in the chair, not the beautician or stylist who is standing behind it."

Bonus Points and Winning Ways

1. **Avoid business boredom:**

    Don't sign letters with the standard, traditional yawners like:
    Sincerely, Cordially, or Very truly yours

    For example, my letters are signed:
    Creatively yours

    And my dad, who is a tax attorney, signs his letters:
    Tax savingly yours

    I know a loan officer in Dallas, who signs:
    Your Texas Loan Star

2. **Use a P.S. and even a P.P.S.:**

    People often read this info first and use it as a call to action (i.e., it commits either you, your client, or prospect to a deliverable—for example, "I'll call you on April 25th at 9:45 A.M., to strategize the next step").

3. **Write a note or a key point in the margin:**

   It helps personalize your correspondence with an informal or folksy reference, and it can also highlight an important passage.

4. **Make it a page-turner:**

   In a multipage letter, don't complete a key thought on a page. Instead stop in midsentence, requiring the reader to flip to the next page (this creates momentum and progress-in-print).

5. **The one-page myth:**

   Don't feel obligated to get lots of information on a single page; the theory that one won't read longer content is absurd (more on this topic in the next Profit Point).

   Plus, a crowded page with lots of text is claustrophobic; it confuses and tires the eye. Instead, give one's eyes the opportunity to dance across the page with space and room to move (white space conveys quality).

Remember, you're communicating with folks about their favorite topic, themselves. Therefore, they'll gobble up a story, narrative, or advice that's in their best interest and that they value.

Be distinctive. Be unique! Focus on creativity, not conformity.

50

The good. The bad. The ugly.

Here are examples of the powerful and putrid in print: the good, the bad, the ugly!

First, an example of the bad and the ugly.

The following letter may even qualify for the infamous categories of "dumb" and "buy a clue!"

To this day, it makes me shake my head in disbelief at the writer's ignorance.

June 29, 1987

Dear Jeff,

Since I last visited with you, I joined the Chicago Barter corporation and because I found it to be so beneficial I then persuaded two of our major clients to also join.

Today I write you with the thought that you might benefit by belonging to Chicago Barter! At the same time while I want to be helpful, I am not so tied up in the whole process that I want to stick my neck out further and venture a phone call.

So if you are at all curious as to how Barter could help you, give me a call. Or if you are really curious, buy me lunch.

Cordially,

Bill

Yikes! Let's quickly analyze this train wreck:

☆ The 4:1 rule is violated, it's closer to 2:1 (lots more *I*, *me*, and *Chicago Barter* references than *you* type words).

☆ Bill says he doesn't "want to stick my neck out . . . and venture a phone call." Yep, guess that would be too dangerous.

☆ Bill expects *me* to call him. Sure, like that's going to happen.

☆ And, if I'm really curious, I have the privilege of buying *him* lunch. Not in this lifetime.

Some folks don't get it. Bill would be the honorary president of the "don't get it" club!

Longer Is Stronger

Now, let's end the controversy about whether your sales letters should be only one page long.

Although it's tough to give a universal rule, since a letter will be influenced by the nature of your offer, your intent (i.e., to inform or to sell a product or service), or the size of the investment, I'm a fan of "long copy" for a simple reason. It works.

Over the years, I've been able to convert lots of clients who were long-copy skeptics into believers. They quickly discovered a basic, yet powerful principle about human psyche:

> **When somebody is interested in a topic, issue,**
> **product, or service, they crave information.**

Lots of it!

So words, when they're the right ones, drive a decision. They don't delay or deter it.

In 1993, I read the article "Why Longer Letters Pull Better" in *The Direct Response Specialist* by Dr. Luther Brock. It's still the best, most succinct, logical, and politely persuasive explanation of this phenomenon. And when Luther and I chatted on May 6, 2003, he said, "An effective sales letter should be written like a dialogue. You have to get the reader involved."

Here are some convincing excerpts from Luther's article "Why Longer Letters Pull Better":

1. **Ask any person if he or she will read a long (three or more pages) sales letter** and you'll hear a resounding "No." Yet this very same person will turn right around and order as a result of a well-developed letter.

   Why?

   > Because people want to know what they're ordering . . .
   >
   > Because their questions can't be answered in a short letter . . .
   >
   > Because there's a heap of difference between handing over $$$ instead of opinions . . .

2. **"But a long letter** is hard to read," I've heard folks say.

   Not so. The trick is to make the reading not only easy, but to *look* easy as well. Big difference.

3. **To make a letter easy to read:**

   Use short sentences (10 to 15 words on average to the lower end of the market; 15 to 20 on average otherwise).

   Use short, familiar words.

   Keep paragraphs short (3 to 5 typed lines).

4. **To make letters *look* easy to read:**

   Keep page 1, down to one or two sentences per paragraph . . . *lots* of one-sentence ones.

   Make margins wide (an inch-and-a-half at least).

   Give page 1 an "open" look. Remember, no matter how easy a letter is to read, if, upon picking it up, it doesn't *look* easy, File 13 here it comes.

5. **There's positive correlation** in many people's minds between letter-length and product value.

   The higher the product price, the more words you need to bring in orders.

6. **People buy from people**, not "companies."

   It's tough to come across as a friendly, caring person in a short (often terse-sounding) letter.

   There are all sorts of guiding-through devices to use to ensure easy reading:

   ☆ Handwritten marginal notes.

   ☆ Underscored words (not too many).

   ☆ Subheads galore.

   ☆ Centered paragraphs (key ones only).

   ☆ Quotes centered and set off in quotation marks, even boxed off.

7. **What this letter-length business boils down to** is this:

   ☆ Test.

   ☆ Find out what works for you.

   ☆ Don't try to understand why.

   This is a "what" medium, not a "why" medium.

   According to aerodynamics experts, a bumblebee shouldn't fly. But the bee doesn't know this and flies just fine. Long letters shouldn't work, but they do.

Thanks, Luther. Great stuff!

(Dr. Brock, a talented copywriter and screenwriter, can be reached at: The Letter Doctor, 2911 Nottingham, Denton, TX 76209; (940) 387-8058; labdoc@attglobal.net.)

The Long Letter in Action

Here's an example of how I use a long letter. The following, or something similar, is sent to a hot prospect.

How is the degree of the prospect's "hot" temperature determined? By factors like:

☆ They called me.

☆ They expressed specific problems to solve, needs to fill, or goals to realize.

☆ The depth of our initial conversation.

☆ They requested I place "hold dates" on my calendar.

☆ They are sending me additional info via e-mail, mail, fax, or next-day delivery, to give me a better understanding of their challenges.

☆ They are the decision maker.

☆ We have discussed desired outcomes.

☆ They want to make a decision by a specific date.

As you read the following letter, along the way I provide comments in parentheses to help you understand the rationale of a tactic or strategy and to make it easy for you to see why we did what we did.

Date:	February 20, 2003
To:	Jerry Gables, President
Company:	Gables
From:	Sheryl Kantor, Blackman & Associates, Inc.
Re:	Your Results!

(Plain and simple—results are the purpose of the letter and of the eventual project or assignment.)

**"We have to give our people tangible ideas
that will generate tangible results!"**
—Jerry Gables
February 20, 2003

(A big, bold, and centered quote is an attention grabber, especially when it's said by your decision maker.)

*Jerry, great to visit. Look forward
to our next conversation.*

Jeff

(Toward the top of the page, in the upper right-hand corner, I'll often jot a short handwritten note.)

Hi Jerry . . .

(This is a lot friendlier than "Dear Mr. Gables.")

What do tangible ideas, impactful programs, and yes . . . even warm and sunny Mexico have in common?

(This references specific topics discussed in our initial call, either business-related or personal—i.e., Jerry's vacation.)

You guessed it! These were just a few of the things you and Jeff discussed this morning. He sure enjoyed chatting with you. And is glad you found him via his new column in (name of publication).

(This reinforces the phone dialogue and how Jerry found me.)

Jerry, per your request and as promised, enclosed you'll find:

(He requested, we promised and now delivered.)

☆ Our four-color brochure.

(Indentations help guide the eye.)

It'll give you an excellent insight into how Jeff can successfully help you and your **Gables** team.

(Gables is bold, not my name or Blackman & Associates.)

RESULTS!

(A bold header helps the flow and readability of the page.)

As you and Jeff briefly discussed, the focus should be on growth and results. With Jeff, that's always the focus. That's why our clients call him a "business-growth specialist." Jeff's strategies and principles are proven in the "real world." For example:

(Notice, my *clients* call me a "business-growth specialist." This has far more credibility than if I called myself by the same title. Also, we're setting the stage for real-world solutions and outcomes, not theoretical or academic mumbo jumbo.

Next, we'll share several client success stories. They could even be industry specific. The stories will differ in length from 50 to 300 words. And they could include testimonials, statistical improvements, or before-and-after comparisons. Real folks with real results. Each success story or tale of triumph will have an indented and bold header. Here are samples.)

☆ **New records!** (A simple, bold header draws attention. And folks like to read about records being broken.)

☆ **A monstrous goal!** (Another short, powerful grabber.)

☆ **Explosive production and profitability!** (Short, sweet, results-oriented.)

☆ **$230 million in 23 months!** (Big bucks in a short time.)

☆ **Double it!** (Creates curiosity to see how these results were obtained.)

☆ **Immediate impact!** (Folks want stuff to work now!)

Jerry, as you can see . . .
others have discovered Jeff's stuff works!

Big time!
Quickly. Ethically. Dramatically.

Increased revenues! Increased profits!
Increased earnings!

(Big. Bold. Beautiful. Benefits-driven.)

Jerry, you'll also see:

☆ Jeff's video preview demo: *Creating Profits through People*.

Here, you'll quickly see what clients value most about Jeff—his:

☆ Energy and quick connection with an audience.
☆ Warm, friendly, and impactful style.
☆ Quality content.
☆ Commitment to customization.
☆ Powerful messages.
☆ Sense of humor.
☆ Audience interaction.
☆ Spontaneity.
☆ Focus on quantifiable outcomes and results.

(These are assets or qualities that *clients* value.)

Jeff brings the preceding and more to every program or learning system. He combines his background to create a positive and action-oriented atmosphere. And *that* leads to significant results for you and the professionals of **Gables**.

   Jerry, as you can tell, there's great creativity and flexibility as to how Jeff can help you and your team maximize results!

Creatively yours,

(Not Sincerely or Cordially)

Sheryl (signature)
Sheryl Kantor
Director of Marketing

P.S. Thought you'd also enjoy the enclosed articles about Jeff. They both highlight his commitment to research and "advance legwork."

(An invitation to dig into the benefits-loaded written promotional material, which once again stresses a commitment to customization.)

P.P.S. As agreed, Jeff will call you next Wednesday at 7:30 A.M., to discuss the next steps for success.

(A commitment to action.)

SRK/mct
Enc.

Now, do you need to suddenly transform all your one-page letters into multiple-page masterpieces? Of course not. But the preceding strategies should give you lots of new ways to turn interest into results—and possibilities into profits.

Profit Point

51

Control and impress!

The late Mark McCormack, founder and CEO of International Management Group (IMG)—the sports management conglomerate representing superstar athletes like Tiger Woods, Wayne Gretzky, Nancy Lopez, Andre Agassi, and others—as well as the author of *What They Don't Teach You at Harvard Business School* and a onetime guest on my radio talk show, told me:

> **"One of life's big frustrations is that people
> don't do what you want them to do.
> But if you can control their impressions of you,
> you can make them want to do,
> what you want them to do."**

Profit Point

52

Push, pull, play, and profit.

I'm convinced that communicated *involvement* is a major reason for the success of The Sharper Image. Their salespeople encourage you to ride the exer-bike, jump on the pogo stick, or crank up the CD.

With *involvement*, Land Rover has also transformed the test ride into an automotive adventure. At multimillion-dollar boutiques known as Land Rover Centres, salespeople dressed in khaki safari attire accompany a prospective owner onto an off-road course built in a dealership's parking lot. It includes steep inclines and rocky hills. Customers love it!

Involvement, a simple and savvy sales strategy, is often ignored. Once I was in a music store where each guitar displayed a sign warning:

Please do not handle. If you wish to buy me, call a salesperson.

Unfortunately, this owner didn't understand the psyche of his customer—the musician who wants to make music!

What if the signs said:

"Together let's make beautiful music." Or,
"I'll make you a star! Start strumming!" Or,
"My strings are quiet, bring them to life!"

Involve your customers. Activate their senses.

Signs of Success

I saw these six great signs at Baer's Furniture in Naples, Florida:

1. *This is not a museum.*
   We welcome you to touch.
   We beg you to touch.
   To inspect.
   To ask questions.
   To be utterly and absolutely and positively nosy.
   If it helps, sit and bounce.
   Turn and squeeze.
   Pull and push.
   Peek beneath the surface.
   The better you know us, the more you will like us.

2. *No need to be tidy.*
   The tables are here to be worked on.
   Feel free to spread out.
   The swatches are here to be examined.
   Please take them down.
   Browsing is thoroughly encouraged.

3. *Ask for our help if you need it.*
   Our services are free.
   Wave us away if you don't.
   Our feelings will not be hurt.
   Nothing would make us happier than to sit down and help.

4. *How about these stripes, with those kinds of flowers?*
   We'll give you our thoughts.
   That's what we do.
   That's what we are here for.

5. *We want to give you opportunity to see in ways you have not seen before.*

   To think in ways you have not thought before.

   To indulge your whims.

   To inspire you!

6. *We believe we are here to give you opportunity to think in ways you have not thought before.*

   To see in ways you have not seen before.

   We offer you the tools to define yourself, who you are and how you'd like to be known in your home.

   We will step up and help you.

   We will stand back and leave you to your own ideas.

   We are here to inspire you.

Profitable Pennies

One financial planner I know uses an involvement strategy that makes his client results sessions memorable and profitable.

Rick's clients are wealthy, high-net-worth individuals. They are sophisticated decision makers. Rick admits his approach is simplistic. Yet it works. Big time!

Here's what Rick does: He takes out a plush felt bag filled with pennies. He gently hands the bag to his clients and tells them the bag represents their financial future. He then encourages them to pour the pennies onto the conference table. Somewhat skeptically, they do.

Rick then tells his clients (let's call them Harry and Pam) that each penny represents $10,000 and belongs to them. It's their money.

Rick suggests they push, pull, and slide the pennies across the table to form different piles.

Each pile or category represents the couple's goals. One pile could be a retirement fund. Another could be set aside for their children's education, while another represents a major purchase down the road or significant contributions to various charities.

Rick says Harry and Pam quickly forget they are playing with pennies. Instead, they strategically plan and calculate their financial future. Obviously, Rick's clients are involved!

Confucius once said:

**"If you tell me . . . I will forget; if you show me . . .
I will remember; if you involve me . . . I will understand!"**

**These statistics reveal the full story and value of involvement:
People remember:**

☆   20 percent of what they hear.

☆   30 percent of what they see.

☆   50 percent of what they see and hear.

☆   80 percent of what they see, hear, and do.

So the next time your customers, clients, or prospects want to touch, see, sniff, taste, or hear . . . let them!

Then, watch them buy!

Profit Point

53

Commotion, communication, and Costco.

There's a phenomenon sweeping across our community. A buzz is in the air. Trumpets are blaring. Traffic is flowing. Lines are forming.

It isn't a bird. A plane. Or even Superman. Heck, amazingly, it's the opening of the wholesale warehouse club, Costco!

These two syllables, Cost-co, are now a retail chant. A shopping mantra. They have seemingly activated the "buying" DNA stored in Chicago's North Shore residents!

How come?

Because the folks at Costco are smart. Real smart. They know prospects and customers are influenced by specificity, not generality. There's a big difference between broad and boastful generalizations about:

☆ Low prices.

☆ Quality merchandise.

☆ Value.

☆ Great service.

☆ Convenience.

versus telling your company's story in exacting detail with facts, figures, statistics, surveys, and data.

Here's some of the "gospel" from the Costco direct mail piece that arrived on our doorstep, weeks before Costco's grand opening:

☆ "Costco sells more than 48,000 rotisserie chickens a day."

☆ "Last year, Costco sold more than 50,000 carats of diamonds."

☆ "Costco's 1 Hour Photo Labs process more than 22 million rolls of film each year."

☆ "Costco's famous hot dog and soda combo meal is the same low price it was 17 years ago—$1.50! Last year, we sold more than 38 million hot dogs!"

☆ "Join the more than 39 million Costco members who save on high-quality and brand-name products!"

The preceding is simple, yet powerful stuff. Each statement is what my law school professors used to call "substantive proof" or "demonstrative evidence." Together, they pile up credibility. They stack success. They form this mountain of results. It's persuasion in print.

Costco lets you know, when you enter, browse, and buy, you aren't alone. Whether you need jewels or junk food, you shop (like millions before you) with confidence and peace of mind.

And it's obviously working. Costco's 306 stores are pumping out $40 billion in sales.

Lessons for You and Your Business

1. Positive facts create positive expectations.
2. Supportive statistics from the past secure sales for the future.
3. Previous customer commitments create credibility.
4. Detail and data drive desire and decisions.
5. Specificity produces profitability.

Questions to Consider

☆ How many customers or clients are you serving?

☆ How much of what did you do for whom, and by when?

☆ What's the impact to your decision makers?

For example:

   ☆ What results were produced?
   ☆ Dollars saved?
   ☆ Dollars made?
   ☆ Percentage points altered?
   ☆ Changes achieved?

That's why weight reduction centers stress statements like, "I lost 23 pounds in 5 weeks!" They know weight loss means revenue gain!

You, too, should know your meaningful metrics. Then, tell the world!

P.I.T. Stop

P   Provocative or Playful
I   Inspirational or Informational
T   Thoughts or Theories

Canine Confusion

My sister Linda's first wedding was an "intimate" affair. Three hundred of our family and friends celebrated at a downtown Chicago hotel. However, Oliver, our eight-pound black poodle, wasn't on the guest list. Tammie, my younger sister, and I thought this was an unfortunate oversight.

So armed with white and black material, rhinestone buttons, and silver sequins, Tammie and I visited a family friend who was a seamstress. Our request: "Please make Oliver a tuxedo with tails!"

On Linda's wedding day, I snuck Oliver into the hotel. Then, after the ceremony, I released him to wander the reception area. He looked resplendent in his tux. The guests loved it. My Mom was fuming!

However, between the end of the reception and the start of dinner, Mom "lost" Oliver. She was frantic.

Now, Tammie and I could have told Mom we knew Oliver was hiding at our feet beneath the head table, but we didn't. How come?

Because it was too much fun watching Mom scurry about the hotel in her flowing formal gown, asking strangers, "Excuse me, have you seen a black poodle in a white tuxedo?"

Funny Phone File

Recently, I returned a phone call to a client's direct line, where the following happened:

Him: (in a rather unpleasant and confrontational tone) What?

Me: David, is everything okay?

Him: (somewhat embarrassed and flustered) Jeff? Oh. Um. Am really sorry. I must be losing my mind. I thought this was my cell phone and you were my mother. And she's the last person I wanted to talk to!

"The difference between perseverance and obstinacy is that one often comes from a strong will, and the other from a strong won't."

—*Henry Ward Beecher*

Profit Pillar

VI

Referrals:
Your Road
to Results!

Profit Point

54

All you have to do is ask!

It's an untapped market. It's a lead with virtually no acquisition cost. It's an abundance of opportunity. And all you have to do is ask!

It's the power and profit—of referrals!

**When your customers, clients, and prospects
know you, like you, and trust you,
they will willingly refer you to others.**

Why? Because they value what you and your company bring to the table. And since you have a commitment to *service*, it's a *disservice* not to see how you can help one's family, friends, co-workers, and business associates attain a more favorable future. Let me repeat that . . .

If you don't ask for referrals, it's:

☆ A disservice   ☆ A service debacle

☆ A marketing faux pas   ☆ A profit boo-boo

☆ A sales blunder   ☆ A commission catastrophe

☆ A revenue mistake   ☆ An earnings error

Well, okay, it's just plain dumb. And you ain't dumb!

187

> **Without referrals, you're unintentionally neglecting
> hundreds or even thousands of potential customers
> or clients, and innocently bypassing
> millions of dollars in potential business.**

A study by the Mortgage Bankers Association of America once revealed:

> Those searching for mortgages are influenced most by advice
> from friends and family. More than one-third of buyers said
> they rely on friends for guidance on where to seek a loan.

The preceding study could have been conducted by your industry or, for that matter, any type of business. And guess what? I bet the findings would be the same!

Ironically, today, as I was writing this section, I received a call from a friend and an e-mail from a peer, who both asked the same question: "Jeff, who do you know that . . ."

Quickly, I gave them access to others they could rely on—people they could trust.

That's what referrals do. They expand a network and help generate results. Fast!

Here's what some of your fellow professionals whom I've helped prosper with referrals have said:

> "One customer has already given me 11 referrals."
>
> "Referrals help you meet and exceed your company and personal goals. You just have to ask for them."
>
> "I love getting referrals; there's automatic rapport, and it lets me know my hard work has paid off."
>
> "Customers are eager to offer referrals when they realize you were sincere in your effort to help them."
>
> "Referrals are really hot leads. They are basically free deals that lead to higher volume. It's great!"

I love that last one, because it emphasizes every key benefit of referrals.

Referrals:

☆ **Are hot leads.**
☆ **Are free deals.**
☆ **Lead to higher volume.**

That's a pretty powerful combination!

Heard's Herd!

In 1998, I had the pleasure to work with Bill Heard Enterprises. Bill Heard is a name you're probably familiar with, especially if you live in the southeastern or southwestern United States. Their Oldsmobile, Cadillac, and Chevrolet car dealerships are abundant in Florida, Georgia, Tennessee, Texas, Nevada, Alabama, and Arizona. Heard is also the world's largest Chevy retailer.

In 1993, Bill Heard Enterprises was listed as one of *Forbes* magazine's 500 largest privately held corporations in the United States. In 1995, Heard earned its first $1 billion in annual sales. The goal for 2005: $5 billion in sales!

One of the reasons Heard continues to grow is because Heard folks know how to sell. Especially with referrals.

Attending a program I led in Atlanta for Bill Heard's dealerships was Jack Colson, a member of Heard's senior leadership team. Before Jack joined the management team, he sold cars. Lots of them! He sold 38 in one day, and 114 in one month. Jack was even featured in the *Guinness Book of World Records*.

So how'd he do it? Here's what Jack told me:

"Jeff, all I'd do was ask every satisfied buyer and even prospect if they knew anybody else I might be able to help."

With that simple referral strategy, Jack Colson would arrive at work with people literally waiting in the parking lot to see him. They'd buy cars and then give Jack the names of friends, family, and co-workers, who would buy even more cars.

Maybe on the *Guinness* page for world sales records in your industry we'll soon see your name!

Plus . . .

Referrals help you make *others* look like heroes.

Your referral source and referral provider have a great sense of pride and fulfillment when they can turn on *their* friends, family, and peers to *their* expert—you!

You have probably heard others proudly proclaim things like:

"Oh, you have to call my doctor—he's a big man."

"My attorney is incredible; she's the best. Here's her number."

"She's tops in her field; contact her immediately."

"If you need that taken care of, there's only one person to call. He's been helping me for years."

Yet, despite all the benefits of a proactive and profit-producing referrals network—with some salespeople, companies or sales cultures, the effective use of referrals is still minimal or even obsolete. Ouch!

How come? Take a peek at the next Profit Point and find out.

Profit Point

55

Remember to R.E.M.E.M.B.E.R.

A client asked me recently, "Jeff, since you do extensive work with clients in lead generation and referrals, I was wondering—how come most businesspeople don't use this effective business builder more often?"

It's a great question. And you might conclude referrals aren't a more proactive lead generator because salespeople believe:

☆ They're not part of their company's culture.

☆ They think they might offend a satisfied customer with their request.

☆ They've already got plenty of leads.

☆ They consider a referred lead to be a "cold call."

☆ They fear rejection (meaning the request for a referral will be dismissed by their customer or referral source).

☆ They fear rejection (meaning their contact with the prospect or referred lead will be met with disinterest or disdain).

While the preceding might be rationalized justifications for inaction, they're still not the number one reason for referral reluctance.

Believe it or not, countless clients have told me that the number one reason they don't ask for referrals is because . . . they forget. Amazing, but true!

So to help clients—and now you—never forget, I developed a simple acronym:

R. E. M. E. M. B. E. R.

And I urge my clients and you . . .
to remember to
R. E. M. E. M. B. E. R.

R	Referrals
E	Every
M	Moment
E	Every
M	Month
B	Bring
E	Excellent
R	Results

Incredibly simple. Incredibly powerful.

To reinforce the power of this acronym and its application, my clients:

☆ Who earn six and seven figures scrawl this word across the top of a legal pad page as they prepare to meet a client or prospect (this enables them to see the word REMEMBER during the actual client/prospect interview, so they'll be sure to ask for referrals).

☆ Have it scroll across their computer as a screen saver.

☆ Stick REMEMBER stickers to the tops of their desktop monitors.

☆ Make REMEMBER buttons.

☆ String giant banners in their offices urging their team to:

Remember to R.E.M.E.M.B.E.R.

Profit Point

56

230 million reasons.

Early in 1998, I suggested to the senior leadership team of Banc One Financial Services (a division of Bank One) the development of a referrals program or system. It would strategically teach the bank's loan officers to ask for referrals and then convert these new leads into booked loans.

The leaders agreed, yet wondered, "Jeff, how do you know it'll work?" I simply said, "Its success is up to your people. When they execute, the results will be quick and dramatic."

And the results *were* quick and dramatic! Here's a brief recap:

In late March 1998, we introduced the "Referrals: Your Road to Results" strategies at three branch centers. While the initial response was excellent, I knew these positive expectations had to be translated into bottom-line results.

They were!

**Within two weeks, $335,000 in new business
was generated from referrals.
And within two months,
referrals had generated new booked loan volume of $896,331!**

Based on these early successes, the bank's senior leadership team enthusiastically declared, "Jeff, let's roll it out! Now!"

To support the rollout we created a series of workshops and customized business-growth reinforcement tools (i.e., workbooks, audios, videos, ongoing voice mails, etc.).

The bank's loan officers learned how to:

☆ Ask for referrals.

☆ Develop a referrals network.

☆ Leverage a prospect they were unable to help.

☆ Obtain valuable information about a referred lead.

☆ Contact and communicate with a referred lead and more.

Referrals became an integral part of the bank's daily culture—and volume.

**The referrals program, in 23 months,
produced new volume of $230 million—
all from referrals.**

And the size of a typical referral loan was almost 30 percent greater than a nonreferral loan. (In March 2000, Banc One sold this portfolio to Household International.)

Now you, too, can reap the benefits, results, and rewards of referrals.

Profit Point

57

Referral psyche: your mental mind-set.

Referrals work only when you believe they work. Therefore, let's lay a strong foundation or a "referral results rationale" with a series of questions.

Your answers will help eliminate any hesitation, doubt, or reluctance about how referrals will catapult you to new levels of success.

1. Have you bought goods and services from salespeople that you regularly recommended to others? If so, who? How come?

_____

_____

If you're like me, almost daily you might be helping a friend or co-worker solve a problem, either professionally or personally. Each of us, in some way, is a source of valuable knowledge and plentiful contacts.

We know stuff. And we know people. This makes us a reliable resource of importance and significance.

When friends recently moved back to our community (after being gone for 10 years), they wanted to know where . . .

- ☆ To get their hair cut.
- ☆ To bring their dry cleaning.
- ☆ To order the best deep-dish pizza.
- ☆ To find a lawyer, dentist, or pediatrician.

So whom did they rely on? My wife and me, along with their/our network of friends, family, and business associates. They knew we all would be watching their backs and protecting their best interests.

People love to recommend talented professionals (whether they're doctors or sales pros).

Too many people are comfortable with mediocrity. But you're not one of them. That's why you're reading this book. That's why **you're willing to deliver incredible value and results** to those you sell and serve. That's why **others will be thrilled to recommend or refer you**. And that's why **you should have no hesitancy about asking others for referrals**.

2. What value do you and your company bring to the table that others could benefit from? What outcomes do you produce?

_____

_____

Make a list. How do you help others maximize gain? Minimize loss? Improve performance? Productivity? Profitability?

Your answers reveal the real reasons others say "yes" to you. Your product or service is merely the conduit for the benefits and the outcomes your customers or clients enjoy.

**When you help others maximize their outcomes,
you maximize your income.**

3. What's the size of your typical sale? (Go ahead, write this dollar amount down.)

_____

_____

4. What impact does one more sale, per month, per sales professional have on your company?

_____

_____

5. What impact does one more sale per month have on you?

_____

_____

6. How does one more sale per month make your life easier?

_____

_____

7. What would you do with the earnings from these extra sales?

_____

_____

Now, close your eyes. Imagine what you would do with these additional earnings:

☆　The charitable contributions you would make.

☆　The car you would drive.

☆   The vacation you would take.

☆   The tuitions you would pay.

☆   The investments you would fund.

☆   The improvements you'd make at your home or office.

8. If any still exist, what are your greatest fears or hesitancies when it comes to asking for referrals?

_____

_____

9. How will you overcome these obstacles?

_____

_____

Your answers to the preceding questions should help you realize the impact of referrals is significant. So there's really no need to be hesitant, reluctant, or fearful when it comes to asking for them.

☆   **Any previous trepidation can now be turned into triumph.**

☆   **Any previous doubt can now be turned into desire.**

☆   **Any previous reluctance can now be turned into resilience.**

☆   **Any previous fear can now be turned into fortune.**

**Referrals are generated from
competence and character, rapport and relationships—
not from coercion or pressure.**

Profit Point

58

Relationship power.

Every businessperson I meet tells me how their business is a "relationship business" and their success is "built on relationships." Are they right? Of course they're right. Yet there's a difference between *right* and *results*.

When others talk about "relationships" they're referring to whom they know. Their network. Their circle of influence. Their clique. Their internal club.

While that's an important part of gaining referrals, it's not enough. To truly maximize *your* relationships, two key elements of "relationship power" must exist:

1. Your little r.
2. Your Big R.

Your "little r" refers to *traditional relationship-building*. It's your:

☆ Likeability.

☆ Trust.

☆ Humanity.

☆ Sincerity.

☆ Courtesy.

☆ Personality.

☆ Chemistry.

"Little r" focuses on your ability to get along. It's your inherent nature to be warm, caring, and compassionate. You're empathetic to your customers and prospects. In Yiddish, the word for "little r" is *mensch*. And a mensch is simply a good person.

My friend Susan RoAne, a fellow speaker and author (*How to Work a Room*™ and *The Secrets of Savvy Networking*), says:

> **"Every room you enter is full of potential referrals.**
> **So work that room! Your goal is to make others comfortable**
> **with you. Because then they're more willing to do**
> **business with you and refer business to you, too."**

People like to do business with people they like. However, "little r" alone is not enough for gaining referrals and developing new business. You also need to optimize your "Big R"!

"Big R" focuses on your ability to deliver results! Never forget, people are interested in *who* you are (your "little r") and *what* you can do for them (your "Big R"). One without the other brings only short-term success.

"Big R" is your ability to be a growth specialist. You, your team, your products, your services, and your company have the expertise to help prospects and customers attain a more favorable future by:

☆ Maximizing gain.	☆ Providing security or peace of mind.
☆ Reducing loss.	☆ Developing pride.
☆ Increasing earnings.	☆ Assuring satisfaction.
☆ Slashing costs.	☆ Producing results.
☆ Creating enjoyment.	☆ Enhancing performance.

Remember, your "little r's" and "Big R's" cannot be mutually exclusive.

People invest in who you are *and*
what you can do for them.

Profit Point

59

Swing from the VINe.

To be a successful sales pro with a strong referral pipeline, you must be:

V	**Value driven**
I	**Integrity based**
N	**Nonmanipulative**

Briefly, let's examine this VINe principle.

Value Driven

You must always be selling and delivering products and services of high perceived value. In its advertising Lexus, for example, has capitalized on the perceived value, the pride, the prestige, and the status of owning Lexus automobiles.

Two ingenious print ads for Lexus conveyed value like this:

"You're at a stoplight. It will last 20 seconds. This may be the only time some people ever see you. How do you want to be remembered?"

And,

> *"You're torn. Do you park it outside so the neighbors can see it? Or inside, so the birds can't? You put it inside. But you leave the garage door up."*

Is a Lexus worth the amount of money a buyer is willing to pay? The answer is, it depends! But it depends on what? It depends on whether the decision maker perceives the value to be worth the expense.

Whatever the price, fee, rate, cost, charge, or investment for your product or service, you should always, always deliver more in perceived value than you take in actual cash value. Let me repeat that.

You should always deliver more in perceived value than you take in actual cash value.

Here's another key point about value. In the absence of a value barometer, your relationship is reduced to a price eliminator. One more time:

In the absence of a value barometer, your relationship is reduced to a price eliminator.

For example, if your decision makers think your price is too high and is not justified by the value you're providing, they will use price to eliminate you.

And what if they think your value far exceeds the investment or fee you're asking? They may still eliminate you. Why? Because they're probably wondering, "What's wrong?" "What's the catch?" "What's the real deal?" "What's missing?" "What haven't I been told?"

Once again, what's the result? They may graciously decline. Therefore, in the absence of a value barometer, your relationship is reduced to a price eliminator.

Perceived value is an interesting phenomenon. In 1989 a friend gave me a little card I've always hung onto. The card is called "Values" and it was written by John Ruskin, an English essayist, critic, poet, and social revolutionary (1819–1900).

The card says:

> It's unwise to pay too much, but it's unwise to pay too little.
> When you pay too much you lose a little money, that is all.

> When you pay too little, you sometimes lose everything,
> because the thing you bought was incapable of doing
> the thing you bought it to do.

> The common law of business balance prohibits paying a little
> and getting a lot. It can't be done.

> If you deal with the lowest bidder, it's well to add something
> for the risk you run. And if you do that, you will have enough
> to pay for something better.

The second step in the VINe principle is the I.

Integrity Based

Without integrity, truth, and honesty in the business and referral development process, there's no need to even market, sell, negotiate, or serve.

Your *word* represents your credibility, reputation, and character. You and your decision maker must forge a relationship. And there's no quicker way to destroy that relationship than by deceit, trickery, and white lies. Integrity is nonnegotiable.

> **You never lie.**
>
> **You never cheat.**
>
> **You never steal.**
>
> **You never fudge.**
>
> **Never!**

You never reduce your relationship to a:

☆ Mind-manipulating,

☆ Profit-reducing,

☆ Energy-sapping game of . . .

who do you trust?

Reputation rises above riches. Trust overshadows greed. Character commands commitment. Honesty reigns supreme.

The third step in the VINe principle is the N.

Nonmanipulative

A decision maker who is manipulated is likely either not to buy, to buy and later reject your solution, or under either circumstance tell countless others about the conniving salesperson he or she dealt with. And there's no way they're going to give you referrals. Buyers are turned off by pushy, hard-sell tactics. However, **they seldom mind a polite, positive, and sincere approach to persuasion and persistence**.

When I stress a nonmanipulative approach to selling during a workshop, there are occasionally a few snickers and looks of disbelief. Some claim, "Jeff, there's a logical inconsistency! The art of persuasion and selling requires manipulation."

Ridiculous!

Remember:

☆   When value is high.

☆   When integrity is high.

☆   When nonmanipulation is high.

And yes, sometimes even when the price, fee, rate, cost, charge, or investment is high, what's low?

Resistance!

Manipulation secures only an initial or fleeting success, not the highly lucrative and profitable long-term referral-driven relationship.

Profit Point

60

Is it time?

When I've asked your fellow sales professionals when's the best time to request a referral, here's what they said:

☆ During a phone conversation.

☆ While filling out any type of paperwork or preliminary application.

☆ Immediately following a sale.

☆ Days after a sale is made, you should call and ask.

☆ Days or weeks after a sale is made, you should send a letter and ask.

☆ During a face-to-face meeting.

So when's the best time to ask for referrals? Well, there are six answers:

1. That'll vary with your specific sales situation.
2. That'll vary with your comfort level.
3. When you sense the time is right.
4. Any time.

5. Repeatedly.
6. **All of the above.**

And here's how to do it.

Profit Point

61

Before you bask, you must *ASK*!

Long ago, I learned successful people (folks like you) are strong willed, independent, and self-assured—meaning that if I was to claim that here's the one way, the single strategy, the killer app of how to ask for and get referrals that's guaranteed to help you make money faster than the U.S. Mint could print it, your response would be, "Bull _____!"

Knowing that, do you think I'd be foolish enough to equip you with only one lone approach? No way! I'm here to help you succeed beyond your wildest expectations.

So here are not one, not two, but—count them—22 ways to ask for a referral. Hey, if you don't dig any of these, gimme a break! You're just not trying!

Feel free to combine approaches. Play with the language. Change your cadence. Stress different words. Alter intonation and inflection. Design the questions that work best for you.

The key is to find your winning ways and then use them!

Here are 22 potential power probes to earn referrals:

1. Who else do you know who could benefit from our services?

2. Irv, how do you feel about (company) and my personal commitment to help you? (Let them answer.) Who else do you know, perhaps family, friends, others you work with, who we might also be able to help?

3. Sallie, I have something important to ask you. I need your help. (Pause.) Who else do you know, like you, who also has some (financial, business, etc.) goals that I can help them achieve?

4. Leo, as I grow my business, I could sure use your help. Who else do you know, like family or friends, co-workers, or somebody from a club or group you belong to, who I might also be able to help?

5. Bev, the only way I've been able to grow my business has been because of people like you. I'm wondering if I could ask for your help. (Then follow with the language of your choice.)

6. Charlie, I need your advice. If you were me, which one of your (friends, neighbors, etc.) should I be calling next to see how I can help them, like I helped you?

7. Ida, can I ask you for some guidance? Which one of your (friends, peers, other club members, etc.) do you think I might be able to help? Any others? How about family members? Any others? How about co-workers? Who else? (The use of "Any others?" and "Who else?" are very effective with any referral power probe.)

8. Ted, who else do you know who might be able to benefit from similar (reference your product, service, benefits or outcomes—i.e., financial counsel, communication solutions, growth strategies, etc.)? Any other suggestions? Any clubs? Any directories? . . . That's a great start. Once I contact them, how would you like me to keep you posted on my

progress? (The preceding question is an important one to ask. It lets your referral source know you'll keep them in the loop on progress and success. Later, we'll address how you thank your referral source.)

9. Ralph, I really value our relationship and am thrilled you feel we have accomplished your goals of . . . Who else do you know who wants to also . . . Friends? Co-workers? Who else?

10. Norton, thanks for the trust you've placed in me and (company). We'd like to help more people like yourself in meeting their (business, personal, etc.) goals. Who are some of your friends or family members or co-workers who might also benefit from our services?

11. Congratulations, Nathan, on making a wise decision. (Pause.) Who else do you know who could benefit by making the same wise decision?

12. Bernice, I'm very pleased I was able to assist you in attaining and accomplishing your goal(s) of . . . I'd appreciate the opportunity to make the same difference for someone else you know and care about. Who do you know who could also benefit from my services to help them reach their goals?

13. Monica, congratulations on obtaining _____ with the help of me and (company). Who else do you know who has goals like yourself to improve their (business, lifestyle, financial future, etc.)?

14. Chandler, I truly enjoy working and helping folks like you achieve . . . Who else do you know who I could also help? Wonderful. How should I keep you posted on the results?

15. Rachel, thanks for trusting me with your (family's, company's, personal) . . . Tell me, who else would you trust me to assist or like me to help? What's the best way to reach them?

16. Ward, I'm glad we could help you and June put your (family, company, etc.) in better shape for the future. Who else do you know, like somebody in your family or at work, or even a fellow volunteer at (reference charity) who could benefit in a similar way?

17. Jerry, I enjoy working with you. Now I need your help with one more thing. Who else do you know who has similar goals that I can help them achieve?

18. Elaine, I'm glad you're happy with the positive impact of (reference a product, service, project, etc.). Who else do you know who might need assistance to achieve their goals?

19. George, how smoothly has this process gone for you? Who else do you know who would benefit from the ease and value of (reference a product, service, project, etc.)?

20. As you said, Kramer, this is a great decision for you and your (family, business, future, etc.), and since you're a person who takes action to improve your future, who else do you know who plans for their future like you?

21. I appreciate your business and value our relationship. I'll continue to work hard to help you succeed. By the way, who else do you know who could also benefit from our (products, services, creative strategies, solutions, etc.)?

22. Who do you know, obviously noncompetitive, who . . . (Select from the preceding 21 choices to use the language that's best for you.) This question, **with the emphasis on "obviously noncompetitive," is especially valuable when dealing with a business owner or corporate executive** who prefers that you not help a competitor.)

Profit Point

62

Where else? When else?

While over-the-phone and eyeball-to-eyeball communication are obviously great times to seek referrals, there's an abundance of opportunities with other methods as well. I realize these could be influenced by the nuances of your particular business, but thankfully there are no rules, limitations, or requirements. The possibilities are bountiful. The profits are limitless.

Leveraging Current Communication

What current correspondence, printed materials, or marketing channels can be leveraged and upgraded to promote referral opportunities?

For example:

☆ Letters   ☆ Direct mail pieces
☆ Invoices   ☆ Advertising
☆ Agreements   ☆ Web sites
☆ Faxes   ☆ New product announcements
☆ Postcards   ☆ E-mail signature blocks
☆ Signage   ☆ Business cards

Here's language I spotted on the back of two business cards:

Referrals

Are an important part of my business.
If you would recommend me to your
Friends, family, neighbors
And business associates,
I would truly appreciate it.
Anyone you refer to me will
Always receive special attention
And the finest service.
Remember, don't keep me a secret.

The finest compliment I can ever receive is
a referral from my friends and customers.
Thanks.

You should always be on the prowl and hunt for new business. Yet folks have to know you are. Or they'll often mistakenly conclude, "Heck, you're so busy and successful, I had no idea you were looking for new biz."

Creating New Communication

What new correspondence or communication can be created to promote referral opportunities?
For example:

Promotional Products or Ad Specialties

Possibilities include customized imprinted items (i.e., pens, magnets, mugs, etc.).

Special Promotions or Surveys

A friend who is a smoker showed me a unique promotion from R. J. Reynolds Tobacco Company.

It stated:

> *Here is a FREE Salem pen and a coupon to show you how much we appreciate your business. Use this Salem pen and fill out our survey to remain eligible for future Salem offers.*

The survey page said:

> *A survey for you . . . and a friend who smokes.*

(It then requested answers about brand loyalty and purchase habits, as well as name and contact information for the friend.)

While I detest the product, it's hard to find fault with the approach.

Referrals Contest or
Ongoing Compensation Plan

These reward your internal nonsales teams (such as operations, administration, technical support, human resources, etc.), and enable everybody to prosper from the discovery and acquisition of new customers.

Contests that Reward Customers or Clients
for Introductions That Produce New Business

Merry Maids, a client of mine specializing in home cleaning, leaves little tent-cards on a customer's kitchen counter, for example, following a job.

The front says:

You're a Terrific Customer

The inside reads:

Thank You!

To express our appreciation, we'd like to give you the opportunity to receive a check from Merry Maids.

If you know a friend or neighbor who you think would also enjoy Merry Maids service, just give us a call. Should your referral become a weekly or biweekly Merry Maids customer, we'll send you a check for $25.

Thanks for your continued confidence in us.

$25.00 Referral Gift!

Be sure that rewarding or compensating your customers or clients for referrals is cool and kosher. Some industries have got specific dos, don'ts, rules, regulations, and even laws about what you can or can't do. It's tough to serve others from behind bars! Therefore, if you're not sure, consult with an attorney.

Garbage into Gold: Do the Unexpected

Would it be fair to say that when you toss out your garbage, you don't expect to get anything back?

Well, in April 1987, my wife and I received an unexpected note from the garbage man. It was neatly folded in a plastic bag and taped to one of the garbage can lids.

It said:

Dear Highland Park Customer,

We are family owned and operated and have been in business on the North Shore for over 35 years. We take personal pride in our service and encourage you to call us if you have any problems, concerns, or questions.

If you are happy with our service, we ask that you tell your friends and neighbors about us. You are our best form of advertising. Please encourage your friends and neighbors, if they don't have our service.

We thank you for giving us the privilege of serving you.

Stephen A. Decker
Ace Disposal Service

This really proves that one man's garbage is another man's fortune!

Profit Point

63

Thanks, but no thanks!

Now that you know how to ask for referrals, especially from satisfied customers, let's explore how you can still leverage a prospect you're unable to help.

The Prospect Who Turns You Down

To this prospect you might say:

> "Tammie, it's unfortunate we're unable to help you right now, and that's okay. Out of curiosity, though, who else do you know that I might be able to help?"

(Here, feel free to adapt any of the previous questions or power phrases.)

Now, I know what you're thinking: "Jeff, you're nuts! This makes no sense; it's totally illogical! Why would someone who is not using you then go ahead and give you referrals?"

Fair question.

But here's why this strategy works. Notice, I didn't say, "Could you give me a lead?" "Would you recommend me in the future?" "How about passing out my business cards?" These requests seldom yield big results.

Instead, I asked if Tammie knew anyone who could benefit from what I do. When this question is asked, here's what I think happens with the referral source's psyche. Most people find it difficult to say "no" or for that matter even "not yet." They feel guilty—as if they've rejected you.

Therefore, in an attempt to remove their guilt, they're helpful and accommodate your request. This simple, positive positioning often quickly leads to results. I've personally turned many "nos" and "not yets" into lots of referrals and new business.

I Wish We Could

Next, how do you handle the scenario where *you* politely say "no" to a prospect? On occasion, though it may be tough, you, too, should be turning down business. That's smart and healthy.

What are some reasons *you* might politely pass? They could include:

☆ Your prospect has budget limitations or might be unable to pay.

☆ Your timing or availability aren't right.

☆ It's a product or service you really don't offer.

☆ You have defined customer criteria or guidelines that the prospect unfortunately can't meet. For example, mortgage applicants can be judged by employment history, income, credit scoring, or debt-to-income ratios.

Here, you might say:

"Phil, it's unfortunate we're unable to help you right now. Out of curiosity, though, who are some of your friends, family members, or co-workers, that I might be able to help?"

(Once again, feel free to adapt any of the previous power phrases or questions.)

This strategy presents no risk to you or your prospect.

Yet the potential for gain, for you and the referral lead, is significant. Your only real risk is to not ask.

What's the price of not asking?

Profit Point

64

People power!

The next 5 to 10 minutes, if you choose, will dramatically impact and literally change:

- ☆ How you do business.
- ☆ How you sell.
- ☆ How you prosper.

"People who need people are the luckiest people in the world."
                                          —*Barbra Streisand*

Here you'll see your networking, prospecting, and referral generation questionnaire. On your own, *right now*, please respond to the following three questions, either in the book or on a separate piece of paper.

Referrals: Your Road to Results!

Networking/Prospecting/Referral Generation Questionnaire

1. **Whom do you know (either an individual or the company they work for or own) who might benefit from your products and/or services?**

(Simply check the appropriate categories.)

___ friend	___ neighbor
___ former employer	___ sorority sister/fraternity
___ relative	brother
___ athletic team member	___ sibling's employer
___ friend's parents	___ spouse's employer
___ church/synagogue	___ friend's parent's
member	company
___ high school contact	___ club/association member
___ grad/law school	___ college contact
contacts	___ doctor
___ landlord	___ vendor
___ other:	

_____

_____

_____

_____

2. **What types of businesses or industries do you feel you have friends or contacts in?**

(Simply check the appropriate categories.)

___ health care	___ restaurant
___ accounting	___ entertainment
___ franchising	___ manufacturing
___ real estate	___ banking
___ insurance	___ law
___ automotive	___ oil and gas
___ retail	___ government
___ high tech	___ financial services

___ other _____

_____

_____

_____

_____

3. **What organizations, clubs, associations, teams, or networks are you already involved with?**

_____

_____

_____

_____

_____

How'd you do? Wonderful. You're off to a great start!

**Now it's time to shake your
O p p o r t u n i t r e e !**

Profit Point

65

Shake your
Opportunitree!

Those who know you and your degree of professionalism, as well as those who are aware of you, your company, its products, services, and capabilities, make for an excellent . . .

Opportunitree

You need to *branch out* and extend yourself!

While prospecting, networking, and seeking referrals, you don't want to waste time. Your time. Your clients'. Or your prospects'.

Therefore, always consider several characteristics (either for an individual or for a market) while you're looking, listening, and anticipating new business:

- ☆ Demographics.
- ☆ Age.
- ☆ Occupation.
- ☆ Length of time known.
- ☆ How well known.

☆   How often seen.

☆   Ability to provide referrals.

☆   Business potential.

☆   Approachability.

☆   Type of business.

☆   A niche (i.e., manufacturing, hospitality, etc.).

"A wise person will make more opportunities than he or she finds."

—*Francis Bacon*

Now, please take a Focus Five™ approach—meaning select five general categories from the preceding questionnaire where you think there's the greatest opportunity for referral success. For example, friends, neighbors, the real estate industry, a charitable organization, and your health club.

Now list one to five names, or more, of people within each category who can become for you a referral source or center of influence.

O p p o r t u n i t r e e
Categories and Contacts

(See previous category listings.)

   A.   **Category:** _____

        Contacts:

        1. _____

        2. _____

        3. _____

        4. _____

        5. _____

B. **Category:** _____

   Contacts:

   1. _____

   2. _____

   3. _____

   4. _____

   5. _____

C. **Category:** _____

   Contacts:

   1. _____

   2. _____

   3. _____

   4. _____

   5. _____

D. **Category:** _____

   Contacts:

   1. _____

   2. _____

   3. _____

   4. _____

   5. _____

E. **Category:** _____

   Contacts:

   1. _____

   2. _____

   3. _____

   4. _____

   5. _____

How many names do you have? Excellent.

When I've conducted the preceding exercise in a live workshop, the results are staggering. For example, recently I gave a group of 54 sales pros only six minutes to complete this exercise.

In six minutes, they came up with 426 potential referral sources. And 254 of these were individuals they never considered before as being influential in or major contributors to their success.

**You, too, should now see before you . . .
a future pipeline of profit.**

However, these names on your list are of value only if you take action.

Profit Point

66

Don't be a sap without a R.A.P.

Referral Action Plan

Now that you have a growing list of referral opportunities, you need to decide:

1. The strategy you'll use to contact each person.
2. The date you'll contact them by.

Number two is easy. Pick the date and do it.

Number one also should be easy, but all too often I see folks make it complex. And complexity creates confusion.

For example, people often want to develop an extensive and elaborate "letter writing campaign." While this is a possibility, it's never my first suggestion. Clients will challenge me with a defiant "Why?" Here's why.

First, it takes too long. You're going to fret and brood over the opening paragraph. Are the commas in the right place? Is it too long? Too short? Just right? And then, three months later, when you decide the letter is perfect, you'll suddenly realize, "Whoa, 90 days have passed and I'm still getting ready!" And, "I probably blew 90 days of possibilities."

Therefore, to save your sanity and maximize your results, let me ask you a question:

If you had something that could benefit a friend, family member, peer, or co-worker, would you write them a letter, shoot them a fax, send them an e-mail, or create some fancy, schmancy brochure?

Probably not.

Instead, you're most likely to simply pick up the phone and give them a buzz. That's what friends do. They yak. They chat. They visit. They kibitz. They rap. They laugh. They get together for a meal, a ball game, a round of golf, or a cultural event.

> *"There are always opportunities through which business people can profit handsomely, if they will only recognize and seize them."*
>
> —*J. Paul Getty*

Therefore, begin to aggressively and intelligently work:

☆ Your referral sources.
☆ Your decision influencers.
☆ Your R.A.P./Referral Action Plan.

Start with your best five. (See your O p p o r t u n i t r e e.)

1. Name: _____
   I will contact them by this date: _____
   Strategy: _____

   _____

2. Name: _____
   I will contact them by this date: _____
   Strategy: _____

   _____

3. Name: _____

I will contact them by this date: _____

Strategy: _____

_____

4. Name: _____

I will contact them by this date: _____

Strategy: _____

_____

5. Name: _____

I will contact them by this date: _____

Strategy: _____

_____

When you have contacted your "best five," move on to your next "best five" and so on. (Realize, though, each "best five" is going to give you even more referral sources and leads.)

**Plus, you should always be contacting
your current or recent customers and clients.
They already know you, like you, and trust you.**

Profit Point

67

Fly the friendly skies!

Here are your choices:

☆ Cloth or leather?

☆ Cramped or comfy?

☆ Service that's hurried and harried or attentive and personalized?

☆ Salty peanuts in a tiny cellophane bag or a meal served on a plate?

When you travel by air, if given the choice, where do you want to sit? First class? Me, too!

Even though the back of the plane lands before the front of the plane, being up front definitely has its advantages! It's no different in the referral and business development process.

Let's look at the four different referrals you might get:

1. Economy.
2. Coach.
3. Business.
4. First class.

Economy

An economy referral is where you get:

☆ A name and telephone number.

Yet this is restricted travel, because your referral source (for whatever reason or concern) requests you make no reference to them.

At best, this is really the equivalent of a chilly lead or a cold call.

Coach

With a coach referral, you get:

☆ A name and a telephone number.
☆ The okay to make reference to your referral source.

This is an upgrade, although it may still be only a lukewarm lead.

Business Class

With this upgrade or reassigned seating, you get:

☆ A name and a telephone number.
☆ The okay to make reference to your referral source.
☆ Crucial information about the referred lead (soon we'll share how you'll get this "crucial information").

Now you're headed in the right direction. Flying at a new elevation. *This* is a warm lead.

First Class

Here's where you want to be seated. With this upgrade, you now have:

☆ A name and a telephone number.

☆ The okay to make reference to your referral source.

☆ Crucial information about the referred lead.

☆ Knowledge that this person has a goal, a challenge, or a problem requiring your specific help and expertise.

This is a hot lead!

To gain "knowledge" as well as "crucial information" and other insights about your referred lead, here are some potential questions to ask your referral source. (The questions could obviously be influenced by your product or service.)

First Class Questions

☆ How do you know each other?

☆ What does he do?

☆ How long has she been with this company? What's her title and some of her responsibilities?

☆ What do you like or admire most about this person?

☆ How would you describe his personality? Direct? Friendly? Reserved?

☆ What can you tell me about her family, approach to business, priorities, or decision-making style?

☆ What are her hobbies or personal interests?

☆ Why do you think he's a good person for me to contact?

☆ What else can you tell me about (name) that'll help me help her?

Information and knowledge are power. Armed with this power, you'll be flying first class. Soaring in that infinite sky!

Profit Point

68

Moment of opportunity.

It's now the moment of opportunity. It's time to contact your referred lead, who represents to you an infinite pipeline of profit.

Here are some conversation openers that quickly and effectively create rapport and credibility.

Success Stage 1

"Hi, Bob, my name is _____. Your friend John Smith **asked** that I call you, and I **promised** him that I would."

"Hi, Bob, this is _____. Your (attorney, fellow club member, brother, etc.) John Smith **suggested** that I give you a buzz, and I **promised** him that I would."

"Hi, Bob, my name is _____, and John Smith sure is a big fan of yours! He told me yesterday that (here you'd reference an insight that John shared about Bob—something he admires, a personal tidbit, a professional fact, etc.). Bob, John **asked** that I call you, and I **promised** him that I would."

There are several keys to results here in Success Stage 1. First, be sure to use the words **asked** or **suggested** and **promised**. These are words of commitment and reliability. They stress you're a person who is responsible and dependable. You can be trusted. When somebody asks you to do something, you do it.

However . . .

**You can use "asked," "suggested,"
and "promised" only if it's true.
Never, ever falsely attribute a referral source.**

**A relationship can't be built on trust
if it starts with a lie!**

Next, don't rush through your opening statement. Take your time. Choose your words carefully. Be conversational. And know the benefit and value . . . of a pause.

In our example, if our prospect Bob does or doesn't ask, "What's this about?" you still advance to Success Stage 2.

If he asks, "What's this about?" your answer, as you'll soon see, is responsive to his question.

If he doesn't ask, the next stage is a smooth and powerful transition.

Success Stage 2

Deliver a **"benefit blast."** For example, "Bob, John and I had the opportunity to . . .

- ☆ **"Work together on improving . . ."**
- ☆ "Help his family or company achieve . . ."
- ☆ **"Increase his _____, by . . ."**
- ☆ "Significantly impact . . ."
- ☆ **"Accelerate his _____, with . . ."**
- ☆ "Produce _____ in (time frame)."

The "benefit blast" works especially well with forceful action verbs like:

Increase	Upgrade	Decrease
Accelerate	Improve	Enhance
Generate	Create	Drive
Eliminate	Develop	Build
Promote	Deliver	Expand
Advance	Strengthen	Grow

Caveat: The "benefit blast" must be short, succinct, and powerful. *Do not* offer an info dump! The benefit blast can literally take less than 5 to 10 seconds.

Success Stage 3

"Bob, John thought that I might be able to help you and your (family, business, team, etc.) achieve similar results."

Notice the use of the word "might." It's a qualifier word. But that's okay. Because you still don't know for sure whether you can help Bob. That will be discovered and determined only through dialogue.

Once you've successfully established rapport and credibility, it's time to probe. (Develop your list of power probes and use them. (For additional ideas, review Profit Pillar II.)

The goal in this call is not necessarily to "sell" and get a thumbs-up, a commitment, a purchase order, or a check. Instead, it may be simply to explore the possibilities or schedule a face-to-face meeting. (This will obviously be influenced by your product, service, investment, etc.)

Here's another conversation opener. It demonstrates all three Success Stages in action:

"Hi, Leo, my name is _____. Renee Rotnak, your fellow board member from The Charity, suggested yesterday during lunch that I contact you. And Leo, I promised Renee that I'd call you today. Renee said you're a lot of fun to work with on the leadership committee.

"She also said that, like her, you're focused on results. This past quarter, we helped Renee and her company increase sales by 24.7 percent in only three months! And Renee thought we should visit, to see how I could help you, too, grow your business."

Here's one more conversation opener. It, too, demonstrates all three Success Stages in action. Plus, it plants the referral seed.

"Hi, Oprah, my name is _____. Your friend, Dave Ledermin, suggested I call you, and I promised him that I would. Recently, I had the opportunity to help Dave and his company reduce their sales cycle by four months, while increasing their conversion ratio from 2 out of 9 to 5 out of 9 and elevating their average sale by 23 percent.

Oprah, Dave was very happy with his dramatic results and our working relationship. **And since he knows I devote my time primarily to clients who are referrals**, he was nice enough to think it might be worthwhile for us to visit about how I can help you and your growing business, too."

(Now, briefly question and qualify.)
Potential initial "phone probes" might be:

☆ Tell me more about the challenges you have in growing your business.

☆ What are your priorities?

☆ What would you like to accomplish with . . . ?

☆ What's most important to you about . . . ?

☆ When it comes to _____, what would you like to . . . ?

The preceding are questions you could ask during your first phone call. However, they may not be necessary. Remember, your goal is likely to be the face-to-face meeting.

Here are five sample power probes used by a client of mine in financial services (i.e., debt-consolidation and home loans). These five questions are asked of applicants over the phone, because the client's loan officers never have eyeball-to-eyeball contact with customers.

1. What's your biggest challenge in handling your debt?
2. What's most important to you: becoming debt-free quicker, reducing monthly out-of-pocket expenses, or both? How come?
3. What are your financial goals? How can I help you get there?
4. What does your perfect financial picture look like?
5. What major expenses do you anticipate over the next 12 months?

The preceding questions and others are used to quickly convert referred leads into qualified prospects (i.e., the application process begins during this first call).

Keep your power probes next to your telephone, in your briefcase, in a file in your computer, and on audiotape or CD. Keep them close, so they're easy to see, easy to ask, and easy to benefit from.

Probing opens your door to opportunity and success. Remember, your ability to probe, to examine, to inquire, and to thoroughly investigate is one of your most important and profit-producing business-growth tools.

And probing enables you to get referrals, convert referrals, and reap referral rewards.

R.E.M.E.M.B.E.R.

REFERRALS EVERY MOMENT EVERY MONTH
BRING EXCELLENT RESULTS

Profit Point

69

It's great to give!

So what's the best way to thank someone who gives you a referral?

For the initial introduction, a "thank you" (via the phone, a handwritten note, or even e-mail) is simple and effective.

And how about when that introduction leads to a new customer or client?

Here's where the fun begins. Because it gives you the opportunity to personalize a gift (if you choose) based on the referral source's hobbies, interests, and even charitable endeavors.

For example, to thank referral sources, some of the things I've done include:

☆ Sending unique crystal figurines (of a golfer or another object of significance or symbolism).

☆ Sending exotic and unique flower arrangements.

☆ Making a donation in the referral source's name to their favorite charity.

☆ Treating them to dinner at their favorite five-star restaurant.

Where appropriate, you can even consider a more formalized arrangement, with a commission being paid for referral introductions and booked business. This is obviously not a common practice with friends, clients, or family. However, it can be a consideration with other professionals, business peers, or service providers.

While a gift, especially one that's meaningful to the one who referred you, is always a winner, something as simplistic as a heartfelt note
can also be very impactful.

Here's an example. Since 1993, I've been recommending Evelyn
Zuehlke to my family, friends, and clients. She's more than a chiropractor; she's my miracle worker! When I've been bent over in pain, Evelyn
has always been available to work her magic. (Once, she even gave me an
adjustment at her home on a Sunday afternoon, only hours before an
out-of-town trip.)

Evelyn is an extremely talented health care provider. Yet she's also a
really smart businesswoman. The following is a letter she sent me:

Dear Jeff . . .

Some days, there just doesn't seem to be enough hours for us
to get everything done. As a matter of fact, some weeks can be
like that. Some of us even go through much of our lives feeling pressed for time.

And even though we may have the best intentions, sometimes
we overlook or forget to acknowledge those to whom we owe
our appreciation. I'm sure we've all been guilty of that at one
time or another.

But I have made a promise to myself that I won't allow the
pressures of time and work to keep me from expressing my
gratitude and appreciation to those, like yourself, who have
shown confidence in me by referring others into the practice.

It may not seem to you that referring a family member,
friend, or co-worker to me is worthy of any special recognition, but I take my responsibilities to my patients very seri-
ously and your trust in me is a much appreciated validation
of my work.

I'd like to express my sincere thanks for your recent referral of
Linda to my practice.

And I just want you to know that I consider you to be a valued
friend of the practice and I hope that this small token of my
esteem will serve as a constant reminder of my appreciation.

Evelyn always sends me stuff, too, such as a pen or a mug. Yet what's most meaningful is her simple expression of gratitude.

Referrals are all about courage, conviction, and control.
When you take control in a positive and proactive way,
it benefits you, your referral providers,
and your referral leads.

P.I.T. Stop

P Provocative or Playful

I Inspirational or Informational

T Thoughts or Theories

Fresh Air

One of my favorite questions for flight attendants is: "What's the funniest thing that ever happened in flight?"

A United flight attendant told me this gem:

Just prior to departure, she was doing a cabin check when she noticed an elderly woman sitting quietly, but with something protruding from her nostrils.

As the flight attendant got closer, she discovered the woman had taken the audio cord dangling from the seat pocket in front of her and placed the double-pronged audio inserts up her nose.

When the flight attendant politely asked, "Are you okay?" the woman calmly responded, "I felt woozy, but am fine now . . . thanks to the oxygen!"

Airport Security

Recently, I spotted a guy at O'Hare International Airport who was wearing both suspenders and a belt. Wouldn't this be the definition of low risk?

Fore!

A client, Tom Conroy, is also a talented athlete. However, Tom recently injured himself . . . playing a round of golf. It seems he smacked his drive about 280 yards right down the middle of the fairway. Yet with the force of his follow-through, Tom severely dislocated a finger. How? His finger smashed into the glass. Huh? Oh, Tom wasn't on a golf course; he was in a bar playing a video game!

"Behold the turtle: He makes progress only when he sticks his neck out."

—James Bryant Conant

Profit Pillar

VII

Mind & Money

Profit Point

70

Psychic debt.

Have you ever given a product or service to a customer or client for nothing? Something you would normally send them a bill or an invoice for, but because of the goodness in your heart, you decided to provide it for free? Thought so.

And if you had sent them a bill, how much would it have been for?

Believe it or not, I've had clients give their customers hundreds, sometimes even thousands of dollars' worth of goods and services for free!

Ouch!

Now, that's okay. But there's a better way.

Next time, if you're going to give a customer something for free, something that customer would normally pay for or something with perceived value attached to it, send that customer a bill. That's right, send a bill. But cross out the amount owed and scribble across the statement:

This one's on us!

No payment due!

No charge!

Complimentary: part of our commitment to always serve you!

This language quickly and powerfully conveys the message that your customer could have paid this actual amount, but instead, the amount is now saved.

Why is this approach so effective?

First, it lets your customer know you made an actual investment of time or money to provide a product or service. Second, it diminishes the potential your decision maker will always expect to get something for nothing. But most important, what this strategy really does is create in a demonstrable way a business advantage with a unique name I know you'll like.

This strategy is called *psychic debt*. And the satisfaction of that debt is likely to have a significantly greater value over the long-term future of your business, than the few extra dollars you might have placed in your bank account now, from the payment of that one bill.

> *Psychic debt* **creates a psychological sense of commitment or loyalty to you and your business.**

Here's one way I counseled a distributor client, Joe, about *psychic debt*:

Joe told me he was providing free delivery to his customers. And if he charged a delivery fee, some of his customers would be paying well in excess of $1,000 a month. Once Joe understood and applied the concept of *psychic debt*, he then sent his customers monthly, quarterly, and yearly transportation or delivery invoices. The actual amounts they could have paid were crossed out. Customers now saw, on a regular basis, Joe truly was providing them with incredible value and tangible dollar savings.

Does the concept of psychic debt apply only to a product? Of course not. It also applies to your time through consulting, training, or the offering of a service. If you provide a client with, let's say, three hours of valuable guidance or training at no charge, assign a dollar value to that service and then send—*a psychic-debt bill!*

Winning Ways

1. Don't give away stuff for nothing. Always convey value.
2. Assign a value to your products or services.
3. Send an invoice to stress that value.
4. Cross off the amount and write a "value message."
5. Realize psychic debt can be far more valuable than actual debt.

Profit Point

71

The 1% Solution™

One of the smartest guys I know is Alan Weiss. He's a talented author, speaker, and consultant. And he's also a valued friend, whom I can regularly rely upon for "Weiss' Wisdom"!

Here's a classic example. Its power is in its simplicity:

**"Improve by 1% a day, and in 70 days
you're twice as good!"**

Wow! How's that for an eye-opener?!

Think of the impact, if you improved just 1% daily in:

☆ Your product knowledge.

☆ Your sales skills.

☆ Your service skills.

☆ Your prospecting skills.

☆ Your referral and lead generation skills.

☆ Your relationship building skills.

☆ Your negotiating skills.

☆ Your follow-up skills.

☆ Your marketing skills.

The 1% Solution is a trademark of the Summit Consulting Group and Alan Weiss, author of *The Ultimate Consultant*.

☆ Your persuasion skills.
☆ Your self-management skills.

Give me a buzz in 70 days. I can't wait to meet the new and improved you!

Profit Point

72

Hustle, hope, and happiness.

Hustle is more than a flurry of activity. It's energy with a purpose. It's enthusiasm with meaning.

Hustle is what drives you to bounce out of bed before the roosters are crowing. It's what allows you to decide at 5:00 P.M. that your day isn't over—it's just beginning.

Hustle is what lets your head hit the pillow—pooped, but proud and fulfilled.

Hustle is defining a prospect's "no" as "not yet." Hustle is always being in the hunt, always playing in the arena. You're an active and aggressive participant, not a casual spectator. You're in the action. You drive the outcome. You make things happen.

When you hustle, the thrill is in your journey, your adventure, your pursuit—as well as reaching your destination.

Your hustle defies the odds. It's polite persistence. It's early mornings and late nights. It's travel. It's time. It's tenacity. It's triumph!

Hustle breeds hope and happiness.

Profit Point

73

Focus versus fear!

So what's one of the greatest contributors to your success?

What's one of your main obstacles?

The answer to the first question is something you must possess. And that's focus.

The answer to the second question is something you must overcome. And that's fear.

When it comes to focus, most folks start their day with self-talk that goes something like this: "What am I going to do?" or "I wonder what's going to happen today?!"

From the moment their eyes open and their feet hit the ground, they are the day's humble servant. They don't attack their day. Instead, they allow the day to attack them. Their day lacks clarity. It's unplanned. It's unstructured. And all too often, it's unproductive and unprofitable.

Focus gives you a distinct vision—for your day and for your life. **Focus helps you:**

☆ **Be decisive and take action.**
☆ **Make today a breakout performance.**
☆ **Light the fire in your belly.**
☆ **Produce the passion in your gut.**
☆ **Live a life of no regrets.**
☆ **Imagine your world of infinite possibilities.**

However, focus is destroyed by fear. Fear can turn the courageous into cowards, the strong into the weak, and the powerful into the pitiful.

To fight fear, stare it in the face. Understand it. Respect it. Acknowledge it. Yet don't fall prey to its menacing allure and evil grasp. Turn your trepidation into triumph, your doubt into desire, and your reluctance into resilience.

Don't let fear fool you. Be willing to walk to the edge. Climb to a higher step. Pursue the path never taken. Ignore the predictors of doom and gloom—the naysayers and the critics. Opposition is often a clue you're on the right track.

See the fear. Then, take action. Stomp on it. Beat it. Whip it. Defeat it. Destroy it. Emerge victorious. Feel the freedom. Turn your fear into focus and fortune.

Profit Point

74

Savor the S.A.B.E.R.

Have you ever heard the figurative business suggestions to "sharpen your ax" or "polish your tools"? Me, too. Well, now I'm gonna suggest that you also wield your saber. Or S.A.B.E.R.!

A saber has a slightly curved blade that's sharp on one edge. It's a powerful tool. And so is this S.A.B.E.R., which will help you achieve a new edge of excellence!

S.A.B.E.R. stands for:

S	**Skills +**
A	**Attitude +**
B	**Behavior +**
E	**Excellence =**
R	**Results**

Skills

Do you have the skills you need to attain the results you desire?
If the answer is "no" then whatta ya gonna do about it?

Consider:

☆ What are the skills you'd like to improve? (Make a list.)

☆ How will you upgrade these skills? (Will you read a book, listen to a cassette or CD, watch a video or DVD, enroll in a seminar or course, or hire a coach or an adviser?)

☆ When will you start this new road to results? (Commit to a date. Define a deliverable. Take the first step.)

Attitude

Is attitude everything? Nope. For without action, it's merely positive fantasy. Yet, attitude matters. Lots!

And, here's the good news. When it comes to attitude, you're the *one* in control. Total control. Positive or negative, it's your decision. Recently, I heard another hotel guest in Battle Creek, Michigan, mumble under his breath, "It's one of those days!" Heck, it was only 10:00 A.M.! Yet he was already convinced he could place this Monday on the losing side of his "daily scorecard."

So what might influence your attitude?

Do you see:

☆ Challenge or opportunity?

☆ Problem or inconvenience?

☆ Dilemma or lesson?

☆ Breakdown or breakthrough?

☆ Mistake or asset?

☆ Failure or fortune?

It's a choice. And the choice is yours!

A sign in a University of Washington oceanography class proclaims:

Man is 97% water; the rest is all attitude.

Behavior

Plain and simple, it's what you do. Not what you promise. Not what you claim. Not what you boast. Not what you intend. But what you *do*.

And all too often, folks aren't doing the right things! They engage in what my eight-year-old daughter Amanda calls "inappropriate behavior." (I know, the wisdom of a sage at a tender age!)

Psychologists even have a fancy term for helping folks who engage in counterproductive conduct: "behavior modification."

With behavior modification, psychologists attempt to positively influence one's behavior by rewarding new and desirable activities or performance and making the undesirable behaviors less attractive.

Whoa. Simple stuff. Good stuff. When it works. Yet often it doesn't. How come? Because it works only when *you* work. At it. On it. With it. Or through it.

With many, when all is said and done, more is usually said than done.

Don't be a "sayer." Be a *doer*!

Excellence

Excellence is about attention to detail. Doing the right thing. The passion and commitment to deliver at peak levels of performance—not once, but repeatedly. It's about turning the ordinary into the extraordinary. It's about the spirit, the will, and the desire to excel. To win. It's realizing that while speed is appreciated, excellence is remembered. Yet to pursue excellence takes guts. For you'll always be testing your limits. As Paul Harvey once said,

"You can outdo you, if you really want to."

Results

That's the name of the game. Like it or not, we keep track. In points. In goals. In grades. In ratings. In dollars. In sales. The simple question, "How'd you do?" is all about results. And results are all about outcomes. Consequences. The tally. The score.

Did you win or lose? Advance or retreat?

Yet, what influences or determines the results are your skills, attitude, behaviors, and excellence.

S + A + B + E = R! A simple formula.

S.A.B.E.R. is a simple tool, yet perhaps an even more dynamic "weapon for winning."

Will you wield this S.A.B.E.R.?

The choice is yours!

"At the end of the game, it is about results. Life is a full-contact sport and there is a score up on the board."

—*Phil McGraw, Ph.D. (a.k.a. Dr. Phil)*

Profit Point

75

Truisms or valuable stuff I have discovered.

☆ Never compromise your integrity.

☆ It's okay to politely say, "No."

☆ Do what you do best. Have others do the rest.

☆ Don't waste time telling others about your grandiose plans. Results inform the world.

☆ Honor your commitments, deadlines, and deliverables.

☆ When in doubt, simply do the right thing.

☆ Be decisive. Take action.

☆ Have a big ego—meaning be self-confident and assured.

☆ Have an ego that still leaves room for flexibility and change.

☆ Respect outside opinion, perspective, and judgment.

☆ Find people who are smarter than you and seek their counsel.

☆ Pay attention to detail.

☆ If you expect a yes, deal only with decision makers.

☆ The easy way out is usually the easy way in . . . to a new problem.

☆ Have a sense of humor. Laugh at yourself.

☆ Ask intelligent questions.

☆ Listen.

☆ On occasion, you will be tested. It will all seemingly be unfair. You will wonder, how is one person supposed to handle all of this!?

You can. And you will.

Profit Point

76

Good-bye to status quo!

My clients are really smart. And fun! Here's proof.

I received an invitation from Rochelle Jacobson, president of N. Merfish Supply in Houston, Texas.

The following is verbatim language:

Send-off party Friday!

Please join us in the downstairs conference room to say good-bye to Status Quo!

Those of you who have been around for a while, know what Status Quo has meant to this place. Through all the ups and downs, Status Quo was always there. So let's raise a glass Friday, November 3, 2000, and wish Status Quo good luck.

Things just won't be the same around here.

So how will you say . . .

Sayonara **to status quo . . .**
Adios **to the way it has always been . . .**
Fuh-ged-about-it, if you have done it that way before.

Remember, life and business are a lot like the organic world: You can either wither and die or grow and prosper.

Toss a fiesta to your future!

Profit Point

77

Fill your pipeline.

Always be on the lookout for opportunity. Shake the bushes. Pound the pavement. Circulate to percolate. Constantly search for new prospects who have problems to solve, needs to fill, and dreams to realize.

Serve your current customers with a vengeance. Yet don't get comfortable. Comfort and complacency can sneak up and bite you on the behind or whack you on the side of the head. It's a bottom-line boo-boo.

And don't put all your eggs in one basket. Things change. Instead, be like a farmer. Till the soil. Plant lots of seeds. Nurture them. Grow them. Harvest them. Reap the rewards. Then, plant more seeds. Watch your farm flourish.

Always be observant. Be creative. Be resourceful. Ask for referrals. Sniff for success. Prowl for potential. Find your future.

Forever, fill your pipeline.

Profit Point

78

Class is always in session.

As a sales superstar, you must listen well, trust your gut instincts, act de-cisively, and have a thirst for new knowledge. Knowledge is power. Knowledge plus experience brings wisdom, understanding, and results.

Your ongoing education is not just a quick injection of "informa-tion absorption" or "training tips." Instead, its an evolutionary process of tweaking, fine-tuning, upgrades, and behavior modification. You must be constantly immersed in your growth and development. Read books. Watch videos. Listen to tapes and CDs. Attend seminars. Surf the Web. Seek counsel. It's okay to ask, "Why?" or simply say, "Tell me more!" Never stop learning and growing. Profits will follow.

If you think you know it all—you're wrong!

With that attitude, you'll never realize your full potential and earn-ing power. You must be a student for life. Be forever curious. Gobble up valuable information. Discover new ideas. Soak them up. Find ways to do it faster, better, and smarter.

Class is always in session!

Profit Point

79

Lessons from a limo.

It was 11:19 A.M. on Tuesday, November 21, 2000.

No. It couldn't be. I stared in disbelief!

Was the long, white stretch limo one lane to my left really going to attempt to make a right-hand turn in front of me?

It kept inching closer and closer. I laid on my horn and slammed on my brakes.

It was futile.

Boom!

Glass shattered. Metal crunched.

I was now an official traffic accident statistic.

Good news: No bumps. No bruises. No cuts.

However, the limo driver immediately jumped out of his stretch and began yelling, "Look what you did to me! Look what you did to me!"

I politely asked, "Are you okay?"

He said, "Yes," and then again exclaimed, "Look what you did to me!"

I suggested he get his license as I called the police.

Seven minutes later the police officer arrived. He told us to move our cars from the busy intersection to a nearby parking lot. There, he motioned both of us into the backseat of the squad car.

He then said, "What happened?" The limo driver began in broken

English, "I make right turn. Go slow—three to four miles per hour. Then he speed up. Hit me. Why he do this?!"

This was a fascinating, yet fictitious tale. I then told the police officer the truth.

The cop, a 20-year veteran, cooly stated, "People lie. Cars do not. Stay here. I want to see the damage."

Three minutes later he returned and reported, "I inspected the cars. The damage tells the story." He addressed the limo driver: "Mr. Blackman is telling the truth. You're not. Mr. Blackman has no damage to the front of his car. It's all on the side, meaning *you* hit *him*. There's no way he hit you!"

The limo driver responded, "Sure, you believe him. He American. I a foreigner!"

Uh-oh. The police officer did not react favorably to this accusation.

For me, a minor traffic accident now became a values lesson.

Reflecting on this experience, was I angry? Nope. Disturbed? Uh-uh.

However, I was disappointed—disappointed at how quickly one can:

Lie.

Blame another for one's own mistake.

Concoct an excuse.

Rationalize a ridiculous reason for another person's logical and correct conclusion.

If you've heard me speak before, you know I continually stress the importance of self-accountability.

If you make a mistake, own it.

If you achieve a victory, relish it.

The only way to attain greatness is by being responsible for it.

Don't point a finger of blame, when it may be far more appropriate to merely glance in the mirror.

Winners make wise decisions. They influence and control the forces that will shape their destiny.

Winners' thought process is:

"What can I do?" versus "Look what he or she did to me!"

Winners are quick to declare:

"I won!"
"I did it!"
"I made it happen!"

Yet, they also unhesitatingly say:

"Oops, I goofed!"
"It's my fault!"
"I apologize. I'm sorry!"

Be a winner!
And, also stay far, far away from stretch limos making unlawful turns!

Profit Point

80

Bravo Leader!

In November 2000, I spent three days at the Saddlebrook Resort, just outside of Tampa, Florida. I was working with a client and its talented team of sales and marketing pros. We accomplished a bunch, and had a ball together!

A major contributor to the fun was that Saddlebrook was swarming with Secret Service agents, bomb-sniffing dogs, and the Florida Department of Law Enforcement.

These were gun toting, curly-earphone wearing, walkie-talkie carrying security pros. (Even the dogs!)

These folks actually mumbled into their wrists and shoulders strange code phrases that began with the words, "Bravo Leader!"

So why were they there? (Well, when I travel, this is the typical security entourage that accompanies me!)

The additional security was really required because the resort was also hosting the Republican Governors Association (RGA).

I innocently asked one Secret Service agent, "So when do the governors arrive?"

His response: "Here and there. Then and now."

Huh?! Not exactly an answer I could set my watch by. Yet I understood the rationale for his retort.

A seemingly harmless answer to the wrong person could jeopardize their elaborate planning and strategizing.

And that's what impressed me most about these security pros: their commitment to detail.

They were incredibly focused and disciplined. They were ready. They were prepared. They were eliminating risk. They had a game plan. They didn't wing it or fly by the seat of their pants!

☆   What's your game plan for success?

☆   What details can you improve on?

☆   Where are you now in your life and career?

☆   Where would you like to be?

☆   How will you get there?

☆   What would you do if you knew it was impossible to fail?

☆   What are the skills, attitudes, and behaviors required to catapult you to your proverbial next level?

☆   What steps will you take to make it happen?

Profit Point

81

Daddy, when do we hit the ceiling?

What will drive you to new heights of success? Is it altruism or capitalism? Is it what you can give or what you can get? Is it selflessness or selfishness? Where will your journey take you?

Several years ago, en route to New Zealand, I was sitting next to a man named Al Wilkerson. Al told me a story that happened to him with his three-year-old daughter Alycia, who was flying for the first time.

As the 747 rolled down the runway, Alycia had a look of fascination and joy. But as the plane started to climb, her face became filled with fear and panic. She kept looking up and then at him, up and at him . . . until she finally blurted out, "Daddy, when do we hit the ceiling?"

Remember, in selling and in life there are no ceilings, no parameters, no boundaries—unless *you* place them there! And when you're breaking through your own mental boundaries, it's not trespassing.

One of my clients has actually placed an eight-inch by eight-inch ceiling tile on the desk of every person in his company. Emblazoned on each tile are these words:

Raise your ceiling!

Profit Point

82

Who's in control?

At any time, but especially during a time of economic uncertainty, what quality is the true economic driver?

First, during the course of any successful career, you're likely to confront some challenging times. You might even experience more twists and turns than a Chubby Checker concert!

Yet the obstacles are not insurmountable. So don't point a finger of blame or rationalize excuses.

Instead, commit to what *you* can control and influence.

Here's a simple example. Since freshman year of high school, Ed Walovitch and I have been friends. And a few year ago he also became a client. (We have both pledged to each other that neither he nor I will reveal to our clients and families what we did as teenagers!)

Eddie will often say to me, "JB, I quoted you from a speech or from one of your books when you said . . ."

Now I get to quote him.

Eddie told me he rounded up his sales directors and asked the following question: "What are all the reasons we won't hit our numbers this year?"

Though surprised by his query, Eddie's team began to fire off answers. He listed their comments on a flip chart. He then asked his team to divide their responses into two categories:

1. Those external factors or influencers they had no control over.
2. Those factors they could control and influence.

Eddie now had two flip chart pages. With the "controllable" list, he then asked his people what they had to do now to turn their thoughts into reality and results. They responded. They got excited. They began to see the possibilities.

As for the "uncontrollable" list, he taped it to the floor of the meeting room in front of the door.

Guess what happened?

As his team entered and exited the room, they were confronted with what they once thought were destructive forces. Yet now they knew these were nonissues. They laughed at them. They stomped on them. They stepped on them. They spat on them. They were now prepared for new victories.

> **Today, tomorrow, in this quarter, and in the future,**
> **goods and services will still be sold and bought.**
> **Decisions will be made.**

So it still remains your responsibility to help others:

☆ Solve their problems.

☆ Fulfill their needs.

☆ Realize their dreams and goals.

Be skeptical of conventional wisdom. Prove the doubters and pessimists *wrong*!

Make *now* a time for growth. And realize it starts with *you*!

For you are in control!

Profit Point

83

Who? You?

So who's the most powerful and influential person in your life? Okay, I'll confess. It's a trick question. There's only one right answer. And that answer is you!

Immediately following a recent keynote presentation, a participant asked me, "Jeff, what makes your stuff different from any other speaker I've ever heard?"

My response perhaps surprised him. I simply said, "You. You make the difference. I'm the messenger, yet *you* get to put the message into motion."

When I speak (or write), my goals are to challenge, inform, intrigue, educate, inspire, and entertain an audience. While it's important each person leaves with an experience they'll long remember, it's more important they attain results they'll always value. That's why I also want to motivate folks to take action.

Information is valuable, yet execution is crucial. You should be compensated for what you do and for what you make happen.

In a time-driven economy, you are rewarded for merely punching a clock or logging hours, while in a results-driven economy, you are rewarded for outcomes.

Now, especially, is a time for results!

And that may require new skills, plus practice, rehearsal, and repetition.

After all, mastery requires repetition. And . . .

- ☆ Repetition leads to recognition.
- ☆ Recognition leads to reinforcement.
- ☆ Reinforcement leads to internalization.
- ☆ Internalization leads to execution.
- ☆ And execution leads to results!

In business and in life, the name of the game is results!

While it's true that our lives are significantly influenced by the books we read and the people we meet, the most influential force in your life is *you*!

What will *you* do to make a difference in your life and the lives of others?

Profit Point

84

G.O.I.M.O.

Always move forward. It's okay to reflect on the past, yet don't brood over it. If it didn't work, learn from it. Then:

G.O.I.M.O.

Get Over It, Move On!

Profit Point

85

A lucky 13.

"What makes a business relationship work?"

A friend, facilitating a workshop on this topic, sought my counsel with this question.

So here are my top 13 thoughts and theories, dos and don'ts, philosophies to embrace, and things to avoid . . . to make business relationships succeed and prosper:

1. The companies and individuals involved share similar core values and business philosophies.

2. The client or customer views their provider as a valued adviser or strategic partner, not as a vendor (vendors are expendable; partners are invaluable).

3. Each sees the other as a contributor to their health and well-being, success, growth, profitability, and a more favorable future.

4. Each doesn't see the other as an interruption or an inconvenience.

5. Each knows how to ask the other the right questions to create the right solutions and achieve the right results.

6. Together they establish metrics to measure success and keep folks accountable (the focus is on behavior and outcomes, not blame and justification).

7. All parties involved honor commitments and deliverables (completing projects on time, promptly responding to requests and communication, returning phone calls, paying on time, etc.).

8. The relationship requires integrity at all levels; without it, there's no foundation for the future (dishonesty destroys; deceit destructs).

9. There's a willingness to be creative. Neither party falls prey to archaic rules, policies, or practices that restrict growth, possibilities, and opportunity.

10. You work with people you like, trust, and respect, and who are fun.

11. There are no hidden agendas.

12. The focus is on value, not price.

13. Politics, personal fiefdoms, or territorial protection are abandoned, so they don't get in the way of results.

P.I.T. Stop

P   Provocative or Playful

I   Inspirational or Informational

T   Thoughts or Theories

Title Time

Actual business titles I've seen or heard:

☆ Master of the Universe   ☆ Dude of Digital

☆ Queen of Communications   ☆ Technology Evangelist

☆ Chief Creative Officer   ☆ Empress of Audio

☆ Head of the Important Stuff ☆ Borrowed Mule

Maternal Madness

I overheard the following at the Kansas City airport:

> Some guy answering his cell phone: Hello. Yep, we just landed. I am fine. Really. No worries. Okay. Okay. Okay. Good-bye!
>
> His friend: Does your wife call you after every flight?
>
> Guy: My wife?! I wish! I'm 47 years old and that was my mother!

Pokemon Pointers

Until you start building up your wins, you are just an ambitious player in a world filled with like-minded enthusiasts. Time now plays a much more important role. So embrace new technologies and discoveries to get the most out of your adventure. Track your progress. And always know where you are going.

—Official Nintendo Pokemon Player's Guide

"It is necessary to relax your muscles. Never relax your brain."

—*Stirling Moss, British racing-car driver*

Profit Pillar

VIII

Serve & Soar!

Profit Point

86

Massage magic.

Ain't it great when the unexpected pleasure slaps you upside the head and reminds you of the little things that really matter in business? Well, I had such an experience!

It wasn't a mere raise-the-bar experience. It launched the bar. It was a moon shot!

A few years ago, I was in Dallas for a five-day business trip. It was the annual meeting for my industry. That's right. In the same place, at the same time, were 1,700 speakers, trainers, and consultants. I know—frightening!

Each convention has commonalities, like loads of content, frenetic schmoozing, the constant search for new ideas, rekindling relationships, nonstop laughter, and, most of all, sleep deprivation!

On day four, I was pooped. So at 3:00 P.M., I decided to sneak up to my room for a well-deserved nap. Then, a better idea hit me.

I approached the concierge and said, "Hi, Machelle, could you please help me schedule an in-room massage within the next 90 minutes?"

She replied, "Hmmm. We usually suggest guests simply go to the health club, but I know who to call."

She reached for the phone and said, "Hi, Sandra, it's Machelle at the Anatole. Mr. Blackman would like an in-room massage at 4:30 or earlier. Are you available? . . . Not till 5. Mr. Blackman, will that work?"

I requested the phone and said, "Hi, Sandra, I've got a commitment this evening and would really like to start at 4:30. Is that possible?"

She answered, "Mr. Blackman, you have my commitment. I'll be there at 4:30 or earlier."

(Smart businesspeople commit to a deliverable.)

At 4:25 there was a knock at the door. It was Sandra.

(The great ones honor their promises.)

She greeted me with a big smile and a firm handshake. She then asked, "Mr. Blackman, where would you like me to set up your massage table?"

(This was now my table, not hers. I suddenly had vested ownership! She used the words *you* and *your* versus *I*, *me*, *mine*, or *my*.)

Sandra then said, "How long have you been in Dallas? What's the purpose of your visit? Tell me more about what you do. . . ."

(She immediately showed an interest in me by asking questions.)

Sandra then made the following request. "To assure you the best results, could you please complete this form?" She handed me a form with questions similar to ones I had completed when visiting my chiropractor or physician.

(Her focus: an outcome with the "best results.")

Over the years I've had lots of massages, but never one that started like this. So I asked, "Sandra, what do you need this information for?" She responded, "Mr. Blackman, the best way for me to help your future is to understand your past. For the body never forgets!"

(Whoa! I wanted to know what time her workshop started! She had a valid reason or justification for her request.)

When my homework assignment was completed, Sandra studied it. She then said, "I see you've had lots of athletic injuries and you're still very competitive with your weekly softball games and workouts. Here's what I suggest: Why don't you take a hot shower, to wake up your muscles. Then, I'll stretch you before we begin, to create positive energy for your massage."

(Who am I to argue with a trained professional who uses ben-

efit statements?! My muscles were about to wake up! And I was going to be the lucky recipient of positive energy!)

As I headed for the invigorating waters of Dallas, Sandra asked, "Oh, Mr. Blackman, which do you prefer, classical music or jazz?" I said, "Classical," to which she responded, "Classical it is!"

(Sandra asked a question that gave me a choice. Once again, she was focused on a simple pleasure to maximize my experience.)

When I exited the shower in running shorts, to my surprise Sandra was on the phone. I heard her say, "Hi, this is Sandra. I'll be giving Mr. Blackman a massage. Could you please hold his calls for the next hour so he won't be disturbed."

(She controlled the environment, to assure success and satisfaction.)

For the next 10 minutes, Sandra stretched me. Bent me. Shaped me. I became a human pretzel. She then said, "Let's continue the healing process. Please lie on your back on your massage table."

(Hey, I was up for healing, especially on my table!)

As Beethoven soothed me in the background, Sandra placed her hands on my forehead and said, "Close your eyes and take a series of deep breaths. As you inhale, take in your hopes, dreams, goals, and aspirations. Visualize them. See them coming true. As you exhale, remove from your life any doubts, fears, pressures, or worries."

(Okay, at this point, I was ready to buy *her* series of CDs, videos, books, and monthly coaching sessions! This wasn't a massage; it was a series of valuable business lessons.)

Within an hour, under Sandra's watchful eye, remarkable business style and magical hands, I was revived. Ready to leap tall buildings in a single bound!

(Business is all about successful outcomes, results, and improved conditions.)

Before Sandra left, we continued to chat about her business and mine. She then asked, "Mr. Blackman, how can my team of massage therapists help you and your fellow professionals at next year's convention? Perhaps with chair massages?"

(She's pursuing the next opportunity, suggesting solutions and seeking referrals. I love it! To Sandra, this wasn't a mere

transaction; it was an opportunity to lay the foundation for a long-term relationship.)

I said, "Sandra, every year, we're in a new city. Next year we'll be in Orlando."

She said, "Oh, that's great. It's easy for me to fly there and coordinate a team of Florida therapists."

(Wow! She even knew how to overcome objections!)

As Sandra left, I thanked her profusely and tipped her handsomely. She deserved it. She delivered. Big time!

(She of course left behind business cards, as well as additional literature on the benefits of her company and massage. Great sales marketers always plant the seed for the next sale. They use a singular positive event to position and leverage a customer for a lifetime of value.)

As I entered the bathroom to shower, I noticed something was different. When I had exited the shower an hour earlier, I had engaged in the "shower dance." You know, that little jig where your feet precariously straddle the tub, one foot remaining implanted in the tub while the other one futilely searches for a safe landing on that tiny bath towel mat on the hotel floor. It's an experience akin to parachuting from a few thousand feet and landing on an M&M!

However, the tiny-target bath mat was gone. In its place Sandra had draped a large bath towel across the floor. She made sure my wet feet would be dry and comfortable for the demanding two-step journey from the shower to the sink!

(She created another moment of massage magic. She anticipated a problem and solved it. It was a bonus or unexpected extra.)

Upon return trips to Dallas, Sandra has continued to work wonders on my sore and tired body. And, to this day, she'll call or e-mail me to stay in touch, to say hi, to simply let me know she's thinking about me and my health and well-being.

(Follow-up breeds success, when it happens after each sale and before the next sale.)

Sandra's company is Mobile Massage. I think it's really mobile success! So the next time you're in Dallas and need a body or business boost, give Sandra a buzz. Oh, be sure to request the deep-penetrating wintergreen!

Bonus Points or Winning Ways

1. How can you upgrade your "contact points" or "moments of magic" with your customers?
2. How are you developing long-term profitable relationships versus merely completing a singular sales transaction?
3. What inexpensive and unexpected extras can you deliver to customers?
4. What problems or needs are your customers and prospects likely to have? How can you offer them preemptive solutions?
5. How effective is your follow-up after a sale? How can you improve it?

Profit Point

87

Hot shower!

Is customer service dead or alive?

Thankfully, in some places, service is still alive, well, and thriving! As I travel, helping companies grow their people and business, I spend lots of time in hotel rooms. And believe me, excitement is no longer generated by a vast movie selection, oatmeal soap bars, or fuzzy shoe shine mitts!

However, good or especially great service stirs my juices!

A few years ago, I stayed at the Hyatt Regency in Indianapolis. It was clean, comfortable, and spacious. Pretty much what one expects from a hotel room. My stay was also uneventful—until I called the bell stand.

At 9:45 A.M., I was promptly and cheerfully greeted by John. He assured me within five minutes he'd be at my room with a cart to escort me and my learning materials to a meeting room. Four minutes later he arrived.

John acknowledged me with a warm and friendly smile. He also inquired about my visit. He then asked, "Did you notice anything special about the seventeenth floor?" I said, "No. Why?"

He then proudly told me, "Mr. Blackman, you spent last night on the Sports Floor!" Surprised, I replied, "I did?!" "Let me explain," John said. "You see this bed. Was it comfortable? Roomy? Well, it should be. And how about your showerhead? See how high that is? Like your bed, it's designed to accommodate a seven-footer!" Now, at five-foot-nine, I started to stand a little taller!

"Mr. Blackman," John then exclaimed enthusiastically, "you see, Indianapolis is the home of the NBA Pacers and the NFL Colts. And to better serve their opponents, our guests, the hotel invested millions of dollars and totally redesigned 34 rooms on this floor to make life easier on the road for these gifted athletes!"

Wow! Talk about a service commitment. John then told me the Hyatt had taken a lot of new NBA and NFL business away from competitors who were not customer focused. Plus, can you guess which hotel the media and fans now frequent and invest dollars at?

Then, one week later (just prior to the start of the NCAA Basketball Tournament and March Madness), I was preparing for a program in a hotel room at Purdue University in West Lafayette, Indiana, not far from Indianapolis. And as I watched the Indianapolis news, the sportscaster reported from the floor of the Hoosier Dome, the site of key tournament games.

However, he didn't wax rhapsodic about state legend Coach Bobby Knight or projected tourney favorites. Instead, he did a three-minute report on where the teams would be staying. You guessed it, the renovated Hyatt with its extra-long beds and extra-high showerheads!

Talk about perceived value, invaluable publicity, and a tremendous testimonial to customer focus and service.

> **When you discover an individual or a company that
> not only meets expectations, but exceeds them,
> you're willing to tell the world about them!**

To help you exceed expectations, as well as devise and execute your customer service action plan, answer these 11 questions:

1. If you asked your customers to list your company's strengths, what would they include?

2. Of all the strengths listed, which three would your customers list as the strongest?

3. What are your organization's weaknesses in the minds of the customers you serve?

4. Of your weaknesses, which three are most frequently mentioned by your customers?

5. What strengths do you have that those you serve don't know about?

6. What strengths do you have that your competition doesn't?

7. What assets do you have that prospects, customers, and clients want?

8. What assets do you have that prospects, customers, and clients need?

9. What's your mission? Or, why do you do what you do?

10. How will you eliminate your weaknesses?

11. How will you communicate your strengths and assets?

Profit Point

Who pays your salary?

Why is it we sometimes ignore those who pay our salary? How come we often neglect the lifeblood of our business? Why is it we forget about the people who help us buy our home, car, and clothes and raise our family? Are we selfish? Rude? Arrogant? Uncaring? No!

Maybe it's just that we often get too excited about the chase, the opportunity to clinch the new deal, reel in the big one, or land that tough-to-get prospect! We forget about the significance of *the customer*!

Today's customers are more sophisticated and more demanding. They have higher expectations. And they can afford to be that way. Because they know if *you* don't serve them, your competitors will. At one time, the deity was greed. Now and throughout the twenty-first century, it's service!

With your commitment to service, you boost retention and profitability. Without it, you jeopardize your future.

Selling without serving is a dangerous game. The penalties are severe. And the penalties are not measured in yardage, points, or minutes. The penalties are measured in lost dollars. *Your* lost dollars.

When you serve, you soar!

Profit Point

89

Insights from the outside!

So how do you get deeper and more valuable input from your customers or clients, aside from traditional surveys or feedback forms?

That's an easy one. Create an advisory group or outside board of directors. Call several of your key customers or clients and ask them to be part of your advisory council. Contact folks who know you, like you, and trust you. And they can also be brutally honest with you, your leadership team, and sales team.

The group can meet quarterly, semiannually, or annually.

I've had the pleasure to facilitate lots of advisory councils or outside boards for a variety of clients. Since I have no bias or predisposition, I can ask the tough questions my clients might be hesitant to ask.

I then counsel my clients to *listen, listen, listen*! I unequivocally urge, repeatedly recommend, and strongly stress that they not convert this meeting into a sales pitch for their latest product or service.

That stinks of bait and switch!

The key is to create a healthy and honest dialogue with your clients or customers, so together you can best determine how to grow your respective businesses.

At these meetings, I emphasize a simple message:

☆   This is a time for honesty, not hesitancy.

☆   This is a time for truth, not timidity.

☆   This is a time for candor, not caution.

The exchanges are always lively, spirited, and even emotional. Yet clients and their customers value the experience. It strengthens relationships, creates deeper levels of understanding, and drives future business.

Also, be sure to pamper your advisers or council members. Spoil them. Treat them like the VIPs they are—meaning pay for their airfare, transportation, hotel, food, and gifts.

Within one to two weeks of the initial dialogue, be sure to:

☆   Send participants thank-you notes.

☆   Send copies of the "team picture" taken at the event.

☆   Send press releases to board members' local newspapers, highlighting their participation.

☆   Send a hard copy or e-mail document recapping the major issues discussed, as well as the game plan for future discussions, action steps, or resolutions.

☆   Honor any commitments or deliverables.

The only risk to your credibility is if you merely listen and choose to do nothing. And that's dumb! And I know you ain't dumb!

Here's more counsel on your council. These additional 11 ideas will help you maximize results.

1. Double your pleasure . . .

Invite two people from each customer's company to participate in the advisory council. (This encourages a shared experience for your customers, plus you and your team get to spend quality time with more decision makers.)

2. Off-site insight . . .

Go off-site, meaning a hotel, conference center, or resort. (A relaxed setting promotes meaningful dialogue.)

3. Be memory independent . . .

Consider audiotaping or videotaping the discussion, or at the very least assign somebody within your organization to take great notes. (This assures that ideas and issues are preserved and understood, plus it makes the follow-up process significantly easier.)

4. Go with a pro . . .

Invest in an experienced facilitator who stimulates ideas and dialogue with humor, spontaneity, and incisive questioning skills. (Do not have somebody from your team lead the discussion, for two reasons: First, it's tough for that person to remain impartial, and second, your customers assume, rightly or wrongly, that there's an agenda or bias.)

5. Team talk . . .

Set up the room with round tables, with approximately four to six people per table and all chairs facing front. (This arrangement fosters a true "roundtable discussion" with direct sight lines or eye contact to table teammates; also, if possible, be sure to have at least one member of your team at each table whose primary role is to *listen*.)

6. Mood music . . .

As you kick off the dialogue, head into a break, or restart after a break, keep the mood upbeat and lively with strong and powerful music.

7. Not here, there . . .

Keep your refreshment tables outside of the room. (This eliminates competing with folks who need to grab one more cup of coffee or being distracted by the waitstaff bursting in and disrupting a meaningful moment with a rumbling cart stacked high with ice and sodapop.)

8. Research rocks . . .

Conduct research; know in advance what's on the minds of your customers and clients. (Prior to actually facilitating clients' councils, I interview via phone several of the attendees, as well as create a simple e-mail questionnaire.) This helps me and my clients identify trends, issues, challenges, and opportunities.)

9. Quality questions . . .

Create specific questions you'd like your customers to discuss during the actual dialogue, yet be flexible enough to head in a new direction quickly, based on the input shared and emotions expressed.

10. Keep the keepers . . .

Have a flip chart for each table, so ideas can be jotted down and posted around the room. (Fill the walls with ideas. This shows progress and possibilities for the future and keeps folks involved and engaged.)

11. Online bottom line . . .

Have an advisory council link at your web site. (It can feature council members, pictures, recaps, updates, etc.)

If you have additional questions about format, timing, scheduling, planning, or creating an advisory council or outside board for your company, please give me a buzz or shoot me an e-mail, so we can explore the possibilities.

**As my clients have learned, the investment for
an outside board is minimal. The results and outcomes
are significant—yet only when you
make the commitment to execution and follow-up.**

Profit Point

90

Tales of terror!

A client recently asked me, "Jeff, what are the worst things you have ever seen a sales or businessperson do?"

Yikes! Just remembering these tales of terror sends shivers down my spine!

Okay, the following may be weird, frightening, and painful, yet they are all true!

Believe it or not and I'm not kidding, from the simple faux pas

to the unforgivable, here are some of the acts I've seen or heard business buffoons and sales slobs commit:

- ☆ Tell dirty jokes.
- ☆ Ignore ringing telephones.
- ☆ Stare at customers, yet not greet them.
- ☆ Leave french fries, half-eaten burgers, and open mustard containers in the sales or display area.
- ☆ Be sloppily attired.
- ☆ B.s. with other employees while ignoring customers.
- ☆ Clean their nails.
- ☆ Complain about their work, company, and leaders.
- ☆ Lie.
- ☆ Read a book, play a game, watch television, or stay glued to their computers while eager customers wait to be served.
- ☆ Argue with customers.
- ☆ Talk with food or a pen in their mouths.
- ☆ Frequently glance at their watch while with customers.
- ☆ Open their mail.
- ☆ Smoke and flick ashes on their office carpets.
- ☆ Refuse to help a customer because they were on break or headed to lunch.

And here's the funniest thing a salesman recently did while his cell phone was ringing:

Me: Would you like to get that?

Him: No! I never answer my cell phone when I'm with a customer!

Me: That's okay.

Him: Nope. You have my total attention. I'm here just for you. Although let me check caller ID to see if it's my wife. Oops. It is. I'll be right back!

Plus, here's the funniest thing a saleswoman said to my wife:

My wife: Hi, could you please help me?

Her: Oh, sorry for the wait. It's so slow and I didn't expect to see anybody today. The mall is dead!

My wife: Well, I'm alive!

Her: Hmmm. Yes, yes, you are!

Do you recognize yourself or one of your teammates in any of the preceding examples? Hope not!

Because . . .

You and your fellow sales pros—and for that matter, everybody in your organization—are walking, talking billboards for your company.

Customers often make hasty generalizations like "Whoa, if that guy is such a jerk, bet everybody in this place is a jerk!" Hey, who said this is fair?! It's tough to create a "wow" when you're perceived as weak or whiny.

What are some of the bizarre behaviors you've seen? Please send them to jeff@jeffblackman.com and we'll add them to the next tally of terror, and give you credit for sharing them.

Profit Point

91

Anniversary angst!

If a twenty-fifth wedding anniversary is silver, then the twentieth must be the year of the Ford Windstar! Huh?!

In 2002, my wife and I celebrated our twentieth anniversary. So how did we spend it? With caviar, candlelight, and soft music? What, are you kidding?!

With three kids, romance is replaced by necessity—like shopping for a new minivan. I know—frightening!

Hey, who needs romance when you've got the sensuality of automatic sliding doors and the family security package?! Now, what's especially interesting about *this* Windstar is what happened after the sale.

Within two weeks, we received a letter from Ford stating:

Congratulations on your purchase. We thank you for your business and intend to make your ownership experience as special as the vehicle itself. Included with this letter is a set of two deluxe foldout chairs, packaged for your convenience in an easy-to-carry tote. The new custom chairs will make any sporting event, camp outing, tailgate party, or leisure activity more pleasurable.

We wish you many years of enjoyment both with your new Ford Windstar and unique custom chairs.

Then, two weeks later, Ford sent us touch-up paint to remedy any accidental bumps and bruises. (For the van. Not us!)

Whoa! Cool stuff!

These are classic examples of "lagniappe," a Louisiana French word or Cajun idiom meaning an unexpected extra.

Lagniappe (pronounced "lan-YAP") is the baker's dozen. The bonus donut. The fabulous freebie. It's just a wee bit more. The surprise gift. The unanticipated goodie.

The Acadians first brought this practice to New Orleans, Louisiana, when they sold grain to their customers in a woolen cloth called *la nappe*. To compensate for grain that might spill or stick to the bottom, the Acadians threw in a little more without charge. They'd exclaim, *"C'est pour la nappe"* ("This is for that caught in the sack.").

In Nawlins (a.k.a. New Orleans), store owners still offer "lagniappe" to deepen friendships, breed goodwill, and generate repeat customers.

For impact, lagniappe need not be expensive. Yet it should be an add-on that's meaningful, memorable, and purposeful.

Folks wax rhapsodic about "value-added." Yet all too often, it's "value-dreaded"! For if the "value-add" doesn't improve, enhance, or upgrade one's life or business, it generates a ho-hum, who-cares shrug.

Recently, my wife ordered some leather goods that included "free embossing," so she requested silver imprinting. Instead, she got gold. When she called and said it wasn't the right color, the owner exclaimed, "What's the big deal? It's free." This entrepreneur didn't get it. She mistakenly believed that "free" entitled her to be wrong.

A lagniappe should create simple, almost monosyllabic responses, like, "Cool!" "Neat!" "Wow!" Which is exactly what I said when the Ford stuff kept landing on our doorstep. (Although I'm still waiting for a free Mustang convertible or replica Model T.)

So how can you "leverage lagniappe" for your business?
Here's some stuff to consider:

☆ What extra goodie (that's part of your service or product mix) can you give with a sale, purchase, or approval?

☆ How will it create a sense of delight or appreciation?

☆ Who can you strategically partner with (to offer their product or service) as a lagniappe, because it complements your product or service?

For example, here's what one of my kitchen and bath showroom clients did:

When their design and remodeling team was creating havoc, dust, and debris with the installation of new countertops, cabinets, and appliances, they'd give homeowners free massages to eliminate stress.

☆ What type of word-of-mouth praise will your lagniappe generate?

☆ Is your lagniappe meaningless or meaningful?

☆ Is it consumable or memorable? (While extra donuts can be yummy, when they're gone, they're forgotten. However, Ford's foldout chairs, for example, have longevity. And whenever we plop down in them, they're subtle reminders and reinforcers of the Ford experience. Try to offer something that's purposeful with permanence.)

☆ What's the risk and real cost of delivering *no* lagniappe?

Oh, by the way, as I have unfortunately and repeatedly discovered, it's impossible to hop out of a minivan and look cool!

Profit Point

92

Customer in training.

As I was about to exit a new local grocery story, I smiled.

How come?

Because next to the perfectly lined rows of shiny steel grocery carts were five minicarts. They were designed just for kids who could accompany moms and dads on supermarket adventures.

And attached to each kid-cart was a sign stating:

Customer in training.

My initial reaction: "That's a cute and clever marketing strategy."

And then *boom*, it hit me!

Billions of dollars are invested in customer service training. It's a focus area I, too, speak, write, and consult on.

However, I know of no seminars that teach customers how to become great customers—up until now!

Therefore, this is the first official declaration of my *Customer in Training* program!

Now I'll teach you, your customers, and your clients 18 ways to become great!

Great Customers and Clients

1. Honor their commitments.
2. Clearly define goals and expectations.

3. Quickly identify the real decision maker.

4. Pay their bills on time.

5. Do not allow you to fall prey to their internal politics.

6. Focus on value and outcomes, not price and discounts.

7. Seek long-term relationships.

8. Desire advisers, not vendors.

9. Enthusiastically provide referrals.

10. Consider you a contribution, not an intrusion to their success.

11. Tell you the truth and never attempt to deceive you.

12. Provide honest feedback.

13. Respect your time.

14. Do not make you jump through hoops, unless it serves a purpose.

15. Respect candor.

16. Return phone calls and reply to e-mails.

17. Value your expertise and opinion.

18. Do not string you along with false promises or expectations.

How do these apply to your customer(s) or client(s)? If your mind and tummy tell you that you have one who is ungrateful and unprofitable, then politely and gracefully move on and don't worry about it.

Find and cherish great customers. And be a great customer, too!

Profit Point

93

No-no. Yeah-yeah!

In responding to prospects, customers, or clients, never say:

1. "You don't understand . . ."
2. **"I'm really busy—you'll just have to wait . . ."**
3. "As I told you before . . ."
4. **"I don't have to listen to this . . ."**
5. "You can't be serious . . ."
6. **"We can't do that and we won't do that because . . ."**
7. "No problem!" (When it's really a big problem!)
8. **"Trust me!"**
9. "You don't need anything today, do you?"
10. **"I just happened to be passing by . . ."**
11. "I'll get back to you."
12. **"We're out of stock."**
13. "It's on order."
14. **"Our policy states . . ."**
15. "It's not my problem."
16. **"No way. Impossible. Never. Forget it."**
17. "I'm going on break. Someone else will have to help you."

18. "You shouldn't . . ."
19. "You're acting like a . . ."
20. **"You'll have to . . ."**
21. "You should have told me that . . ."

The preceding language conveys arrogance, impatience, and indifference, which could all lead to insolvency!

Instead, use "serve and soar" language like:

1. **"How can I help you?"**
2. "Of course we can do that . . ."
3. **"You've come to the right place."**
4. "That's easy!"
5. **"Let's devote the time together to find out exactly what you need . . ."**
6. "I apologize for the delay. I really appreciate your patience."
7. **"Do you mind if I put you on hold? Thanks for waiting."**
8. "I don't know the answer to that question, but I'll be sure to find out and call you no later than four o'clock today . . ."
9. **"It's my pleasure . . ."**
10. "Glad you're here. How can I assist?"
11. **"I know exactly how to solve that problem!"**
12. "We had another customer with that same challenge, and here's what we did . . . "
13. **"There are several alternatives; here's what I suggest . . ."**
14. "Our in-house expert recommends . . ."
15. **"You'll really be happy when you . . ."**
16. "That's not what we specialize in, so here are the names of some folks who will take really good care of you . . ."
17. **"It's always good to hear from you . . ."**
18. "Other clients have found it's really valuable when they . . . "
19. **"Aside from that, how else can I help you . . ."**
20. "How beneficial would it be if you could . . . "

21. **"What can I help you solve today?"**
22. "Together, let's figure out how to make this work . . ."
23. **"What would your perfect solution look like?"**
24. "Together, let's explore the possibilities . . . "
25. **"You have my undivided attention . . ."**
26. "I've blocked this time, to focus on your specific challenge . . ."
27. **"It's always easier when we work together, so let's make it easy . . ."**

Remember, it takes months, even years, to find, sell, and serve a customer, but only seconds to lose one!

Profit Point

94

SERVice with a smile.

Most customers and clients are honest, reasonable people. If there's a problem, they seek fair and fast solutions.

Thankfully, we don't often have to encounter or battle the feared "customer from hell"—although, they do exist.

A painting contractor once told me an amazing story. He said he had just completed painting the interior of a customer's palatial home. The home was gorgeous and so was his work. Or so he thought.

While he admired his skill and artistry, his customer, whom we'll affectionately call Mrs. Pita (pain in _____ _____), declared, "While it may look perfect, it must first pass my nylon test!"

Somewhat baffled, he said, "Excuse me, what's your nylon test?"

She then removed from her pants pocket a wadded-up pair of nylons or pantyhose. She rolled them into a ball and said, "I'll run the nylons over the baseboards, walls, crown molding, and ceiling. If there's a snag, you'll fix it!"

Though shocked by her unrealistic expectation, he politely and quickly remedied the few bumps or snags she found. He told me, "Jeff, the faster I finished, the sooner I could flee!"

So how do you handle the occasional tough or nasty customer? Here's how: with the four-step S.E.R.V.™ problem-solving formula.

The steps are:

S Specify

E Evaluate

R Remedy

V Verify

Each step also has three specific action strategies for resolving problems:

1. Specify.

Specify the difficulty, dilemma, or problem to be solved.

Specification lets you solve your customer's problem, whether it's real or simply perceived. Effective specification requires you to:

☆ Know the facts.

☆ Listen without bias.

☆ Reaffirm or repeat the facts to your customer, to demonstrate you listened.

2. Evaluate.

In this stage you find out:

- ☆ Who goofed or made the mistake.
- ☆ What did or didn't happen.
- ☆ What should have happened that didn't.

The goal here is not to assign blame, but instead to empower or authorize someone within your organization (you or somebody else) to take positive action on behalf of your customer.

3. Remedy.

To remedy the problem, you should do three things:

- ☆ Ask your customer what he or she wants or what he or she suggests to solve the problem.
- ☆ Offer your suggestions.
- ☆ Work together with your customer to reach agreement.

4. Verify.

Here, you verify:

- ☆ The course of action to be taken.
- ☆ That your customer is satisfied with that action.
- ☆ That you value the customer's business.

Will the S.E.R.V. formula always work? Nope.

Unfortunately, no matter what you do or say, there are always those select few customers who are the chronic complainers, the relentless whiners. They can never be satisfied. Their goal is to inflict pain and suffering. They like to add fuel to the fire. They're charter members of "Club Unhappy" and hope to recruit you, too.

However, they're the minority. And remember, nobody ever won an argument with a customer!

Profit Point

95

Have I explained this well?

Have you ever asked a decision maker:

"Do you understand?"

How'd they respond? "You bet!" "Absolutely!" "No problem." "You betcha!" "Yep, that's easy!"

Guess what? They may have had no idea what the heck you said!

Customers, clients, and prospects have egos, too. And they like to protect them. The last thing they want to do is to look stupid, especially in front of you.

Therefore, to protect their self-esteem and save face, they'll often boldly proclaim their understanding, even if you have inadvertently guided them into the land of confusion! (And confusion and misunderstanding are major obstacles to making a sale.)

So here's a far better question to ask:

"Have I explained this well?"

This question is a powerhouse. It cleverly shifts the burden from your customer, client, or prospect to you. And that's where it belongs—on your shoulders, not theirs.

Now even if you ask, "Have I explained this well?" and the response is "No!" that's not a problem. Because you can politely say something like, "Oops, my fault! Let me explain better this time . . . how it'll help you."

This strategy is a winner! Have I explained it well?

Profit Point

96

Hawaiian hospitality.

After a speaking engagement in November of 1990, my wife and I spent a remarkable week at the Hyatt Regency Maui. It's an amazing property with impeccable service.

On our final day, we were requested to complete a brief comment card. (The incentive was some fruity libation with a palm tree towering over the rim of the glass!)

One feedback question asked, "Would you stay with us again?" We were thrilled with our visit, yet when we return to an area we prefer a new experience at a different location, so we answered, "No."

This seemingly simple response, set in motion a series of incredible events.

Two weeks later . . .

. . . **we got a letter from Darryl Hartley-Leonard, President of Hyatt Hotels and Resorts.**

Here are excerpts:

Your feedback is invaluable in monitoring our success. I was distressed to learn you would not return to the Hyatt Regency Maui. We constantly strive to satisfy every guest, and I am disappointed to find we have been unsuccessful.

Please accept my personal apology for the inadequacies you experienced. Let me assure you we will work harder than ever to measure up to your travel needs.

I am asking our manager to follow up with you, to directly address your comments. We value your business and hope you would give Hyatt another chance to regain your confidence.

Whoa! Impressive stuff. (And I wasn't even unhappy.)

Then, we got a letter from Werner Neuteufel, general manager of the Hyatt Regency Maui. He wrote:

Guest satisfaction is our number one priority. I apologize we fell short of this goal during your visit. It is through the feedback of our guests that we look for ways to improve our services and maintain our reputation as a world-class resort. I hope you'll reconsider staying with us on a future visit . . . to show you the high quality of service we know you expect.

Yikes! I figure before I begin receiving more letters from Hyatts throughout the world, the president of the United States, foreign dignitaries, or the Supreme NATO Commander, it's time to set the record straight!

I wrote:

Dear Darryl and Werner,

There's no need to be distressed . . . because I'm impressed!

By what? By the fact that both of you followed up to our guest comment card.

However, let me immediately dismiss your worries that our visit was anything less than positive. While it's true we indicated we would not return to your property for a future visit, it had nothing to do with your commitment to hospitality and guest satisfaction.

Very simply, we like to make every city/trip an adventure . . . and that includes a new hotel!

As your founding philosophy states, "If all we do for our guests is to make them feel at home, we've made a multimillion-dollar mistake! That means we strive to provide all the comforts of home, but with a dash of magic!"

Well, you'll be glad to know your properties and people have been providing this Hyatt "regular" with a "dash of magic" for years.

When I speak, I even tell stories about my Hyatt experiences: room service in Minneapolis, the wake-up call in Houston, and now your letters.

Gentlemen, there's no need for concern. For now, I especially know . . . your ongoing passion to please the customer isn't hype, but a driving business mission.

Darryl, do you think the Hyatt Deerfield would deliver desserts to my home?

Phew! I felt relieved and vindicated. Misconceptions eradicated. Ongoing correspondence politely concluded.

Not quite!

Darryl responded:

I was pleased to learn your visit was in fact enjoyable. It was a pleasure to learn of the excellent service you received. Thanks for the generous feedback.

I'm sorry to say the Hyatt Deerfield is not offering delivery service of their delicious desserts. I should know—I've looked into it myself!

We look forward to welcoming you back to a Hyatt Hotel or Resort in the very near future.

Hyatt's president is my new pen pal! Okay, I'm a believer. No need for more letters. Until . . .
Werner wrote:

Dear Mr. and Mrs. Blackman,
Thanks for taking the time to clarify your comment card. We take negative responses very personally! Your letter has alleviated our concerns, but we hope you will return to our "Palace" and let us make your next stay . . . a whole new adventure. Warmest aloha.

Wow!
Here's one more phenomenal and hard-to-believe tidbit . . .
Werner's note accompanied a wooden crate about the size of a minivan. It was loaded with fresh and exotic Hawaiian tropical flowers—anthuriums, birds of paradise, heliconias, gingers, and decorative foliage.
Implausible. Astounding. Classy!
Hey, by now, I knew what to do!
I immediately sent Werner a thank-you note for his thoughtfulness and surprising gesture of hospitality (fully expecting within two weeks I'd start getting regular shipments of fresh pineapples, Hyatt stock options, and hula dancers!)
So what are the lessons to be learned? There are lots:

1. When you request feedback, pay attention to it.
2. Respond fast.
3. If you goofed, apologize.
4. Let customers and clients know how much you value their input.
5. Respond from the highest level(s) within your organization.

6. When a commitment to follow up is made, make sure it happens.

7. Reference your customer's specific phraseology and words. Don't respond with boilerplate language. Let your personality and humanity shine through.

8. Create a positive tone and attitude that plants a seed for the next opportunity.

9. Do the unexpected, even when it may not be necessary. Produce awe and amazement. Blow 'em away!

10. Generate word-of-mouth in others that begins with, "You're not gonna believe . . ."

11. Ask yourself, "What's the lifetime cost of losing a customer?"

12. Ask yourself, "What's the lifetime value of gaining a new customer?"

13. Ask yourself, "What's the lifetime value of keeping a current customer?"

And there's of course, one more obvious lesson . . .

Start answering the "Will you return?" question on hotel comment cards with a "No" . . . to see if it'll jump-start a parade of presents. (Just kidding!)

P.I.T. Stop

P   Provocative or Playful

I   Inspirational or Informational

T   Thoughts or Theories

Us Yankees Talk Funny.

Scene: New Orleans, Louisiana. A restaurant hostess was seating me for lunch.

Me: After lunch, I need to scoot to Baton Rouge. Could you please point me in the right direction?

Her: Easy. Head toward the front of the restaurant and hang a right.

Me: That's it?

Her: Yep. Just head past my reception desk. You can't miss it.

Me: Excuse me?

Her: You don't get this, do you, buddy? (She takes out a pencil and begins drawing a map on the paper tablecloth. Then she speaks in a slow and loud voice.) Go past my reception desk and turn right.

Me: Thanks. I'm from Chicago and am not sure how to get to Baton Rouge.

Her: (In disbelief) Baton Rouge!? I thought you said "bathroom"!

24/7/365. Not!

Forget about working 9 to 5. Here's the actual sign posted at the Art Expressions store in Northbrook, Illinois:

Office Hours

Open most days about 9 or 10. Occasionally, as early as 7, but some days as late as 12 or 1. We close about 5:30 or 6:00. Occasionally, about 4 or 5, but sometimes as late as 11 or 12. Some days or afternoons, we aren't here at all. And lately, I've been here just about all the time, except when I'm someplace else.

Room Service with a "Bite"

Me: Hi, what's your soup of the day?

Shirley: Don't know. But do know today my husband is driving me nuts!

You must begin to think of yourself as becoming the person you want to be!

Profit Pillar

Fly like
an Eagle!

Profit Points

97. Forget time management. Manage yourself.

98. 21 tips for the 21st century.

99. To know me is to love me.

100. Focus Five.

P.I.T. Stop

97

Forget time management.
Manage yourself.

Each day blesses you with 24 hours. That's 1,440 minutes. No more. No less. Time is relentless. It can't be stopped.

Time is the essence of your life. If you waste your time, you waste your life. Let time become your ally, your valuable partner.

Don't confuse activity with results. You're paid only for results.

Steal time from the insignificant. Then channel it and your energies toward the significant—your goal, objective, or anticipated result. On the "clock of life" or "watch of winners" the key word is *now*!

Procrastination is your foe. Indecision an assassin. Plan tomorrow tonight. Stay on track. Make every day count.

When you master your time, you master your destiny.

Tick, tock. Tick, tock. Tick, tock.

We often wish we had more of it. We're surprised when it passes quickly. And frustrated when it seems to move soooo slowly. It's the uncompromising passage of time.

Time and your management of it are crucial to your success. Wasted time equals lost opportunities. Lost opportunities equal lost earnings.

The often ballyhooed concept of "saving time" is actually a misnomer—or an impossibility! Time can't be saved. You can't store up an inventory of minutes now and then capitalize on your "savings" at a later date.

"Ooh, ooh, that hour I saved in May, I'll use it in December to extend my holiday hoopla!" As cool as that might be, it won't happen.

Time cannot be managed. You can only manage you!

Take a peek at your watch. Now, pretend to bust it! That's right, smash it into smithereens! Guess what, though the current time is now forever frozen, tomorrow it's still going to be accurate. Twice!

We're all given the same amount of time. Yep. That's just the way it is, though it seems like productive and successful salespeople receive an extra supply. Somebody must be sneaking them an extra stash of minutes!

The real key is how you take advantage of:

☆ The 60 seconds in your minute.

☆ The 60 minutes in your hour.

☆ The 1,440 minutes in your day.

☆ The 10,080 minutes in your week.

☆ The 525,600 minutes in your year.

**There are certain basics of time and life
you must understand and master:**

1. Your life and the value of it depend upon your usage of time.

Each day you have 24 hours. Each week you have 168 hours. You get no more. You get no less. Time can't be replaced or reversed. Time is the very essence of your life. If you **master your time, you master your life**. And to the best of our knowledge, it's the only life you have to live.

2. Believe it or not, despite what you may think, you can't do it all or do it alone.

The work of the world or the work of you, as a successful business professional, is seemingly endless. Therefore, the object of life or you in your professional role is not to race compulsively or erratically to do more stuff in less time. Instead, you want to **learn how to make better and wiser choices or decisions**. Your goal is not to become busier or more active, but to **become more selective**.

3. Your time is fixed.

We can squeeze the 25th hour only figuratively. If you want "more time" for one activity, project, or goal, you can't reach into your "time reservoir." Instead, you must "steal" time from another activity, project or goal. Hey, no one ever said this was easy! **Time choices are tough and demanding. But your rewards can be tremendous.**

4. Universal satisfaction.

Mastering your use of time brings great pleasure in both your personal and professional lives. These two aspects of your existence should ideally be wonderfully and harmoniously intertwined.

5. Time management = self-management.

Videotape allows athletic events to be frozen, isolated, or even appreciated from a reverse angle. But our lives don't have the same luxury. You can't stop or save time. You can't even manage it. Therefore, what you really must learn to manage is yourself. And this requires hard work and determination. **Yet when you make the commitment to better time or self-management, success is almost guaranteed!**

6. Know where you're at and where you're going.

Time-effective people have a plan, a goal, an objective. They are proactive, *not* reactive. They make things happen *for* them. They seldom let things happen *to* them. You too must realize that **a steady progression toward your plans, goals, and objectives eventually returns the most rewarding results**.

7. Important doesn't equal urgent.

It's **important to plan your future**, to meet with your team, to serve your customers, to spend time with your family. A sense of urgency is created when you're stuck in traffic after downing a breakfast of coffee and bran muffins! Unfortunately, all too often, life's urgencies seem to dominate life's importancies. And then you begin to wonder what happened to:

- ☆ Your hour.
- ☆ Your day.
- ☆ Your week.
- ☆ Your month.
- ☆ Your quarter.
- ☆ Your year.
- ☆ Your decade.
- ☆ Your life.

8. It's a process, not an event.

To gain control of your time helps you gain control of your life and work. Yet that often requires change. And change often brings about discomfort. Yet without a little squirming and pain, there's seldom gain. Remember, **success happens over time, not overnight.**

> *"As you get older, don't slow down. Speed up. There's less time left!"*
>
> —*Malcolm Forbes*

Profit Point

98

21 tips for the 21st century.

The following 21 strategies will help you maximize your "minute management":

1. Limit your availability.

When you're in your office, unexpected and unplanned interruptions or distractions can "steal" your day. An open-door policy is fine, but not if it has a negative impact on your productivity and profitability. You may even want to create a quiet time where you're assured of no mystery visitors or intruding phone calls.

2. Concentrate your phone calls.

Consider devoting a certain time of the day to both return and originate phone calls. Prior to each call, jot down the points you'd like to cover, and be sure to take notes during the conversation. Also, try to avoid being placed on hold, but if you are, have some type of "quick work" close by, like an article, newsletter, mail, or a letter for your review. Are there exceptions to "concentration calling"? Of course—a customer emergency.

3. Protect your magic minutes.

Are you a morning person or a night owl? Are you at peak creativity and productivity when you bolt out of bed, or do you demand a caffeine injection before you form multisyllabic words? Knowing when you operate at peak performance allows you to devote certain activities to defined segments of the day.

4. Plan your day the night before.

When you get up, you're ready to go! Divide your daily activities by the types of activities you're likely to perform. For example, each day I look at three types of activities on my "to do" list:

1. *Oral activities:* like phone calls or rehearsing new stories or anecdotes I might present to an audience.
2. *Written activities:* like writing newspaper or magazine columns, a book's chapter, audio or video scripts, my monthly electronic newsletter, developing new material for a learning system, client correspondence, or a special marketing project.
3. *Inside or outside activities:* like client appointments, meetings with graphic designers, publishers, advisors, etc.

5. Waiting time shouldn't be wasted time.

When I find myself with "wait time" before someone is ready to meet with me at their office, I don't reach for the lobby's 1992 issue of *Time*. Instead, I'll review questions I prepared for the meeting, comb through a newsletter for a new idea, review my goals, or even start writing a new column.

6. Know your territory.

If you have several appointments or errands, group them in the same geographical area and number them chronologically.

7. Don't be "stuck in traffic."

I'm still amazed at how many people don't use cellular phones. They are inexpensive necessities. The advantages of a cell phone, especially between appointments, are:

☆ Letting a prospect or client know you're on the way or might be a few minutes late (although being late is inexcusable).

☆ Returning phone calls.

☆ Confirming appointments.

☆ Checking messages.

☆ Quick and proficient handling of life's daily minutiae.

☆ Conveying a professional or efficient image.

Your cell phone not only becomes an incredibly effective business tool, but it's also a tremendous relationship builder. Quick contacts often pave the way for future opportunities.

(When I got my first cell phone in 1988, it was $1,200! But it came with this really cool portable battery pack so I could be mobile. The battery pack was about the size of a microwave oven!)

8. Standardize your letters.

If the same or similar pieces of literature leave your office daily, establish a common format. If you've found language or previously approved company letters that work, use them. There's no need to create new prose every time. However, still be sure your letters are personalized and signed. Some salespeople even number the various common paragraphs they might use in a letter and then simply tell their secretary to include, for example, paragraphs 1, 2, 4, and 7.

9. Be aware of time.

Ideally, keep a stopwatch or clock close to your phone or desk. This enables you to monitor activities and track progress. (The screen saver on one of my computers is even a clock.)

10. Confirm appointments.

Never assume your one o'clock is on! Being stood up is frustrating and irritating. A simple phone call or e-mail message eliminates anxiety and wasted effort. Is there a possibility that when you call to confirm, you could find out a scheduled meeting has been canceled? Of course. But far better to discover it now than when you stand dumbfounded in somebody's office mumbling to yourself, "What a jerk! Why didn't he call me?!"

Also, what you really have to assess is, why was the meeting canceled? Oh, sure, on occasion "stuff happens," yet there may be other reasons the meeting didn't happen (did the prospect think it would be valuable to meet, was there appropriate rapport, did you properly qualify, etc.).

11. Allot time for each activity.

Plan how long each item on your "to do" list will take. This helps you keep track of whether you're on schedule or running behind. This idea is a simple one, yet it's a powerhouse. It helps you determine whether you're on-target or about to be gobbled up by the unexpected.

12. Don't get buried by paper.

When possible, try to "touch" each piece of paper only once. File it. Act on it. Or toss it! (Periodically, i.e., every quarter, purge your files. If you haven't touched it in three months, you probably never will. So toss it.) One of my clients has a great saying, "Do it. Ditch it. Or delegate it!"

13. Reduction leads to completion.

Try to complete a major project or task in small bite-size chunks. To tackle the "whole thing" at once, usually increases stress and reduces quality. Plus, each time you finish a portion, it creates a sense of accomplishment.

14. Listen to cassettes and CDs.

Turn your washroom, workout area, or car into an "educational resource center." The impact of audio learning is profound. My car and trunk are loaded with cassettes and CDs. If you listen to "audio learning" tools only 30 minutes each day, that's 2.25 hours each week, or over

100 hours each year. That's plenty of time to earn a master's or Ph.D. in the topic(s) of your choice!

15. Consider the results.

Before you begin an activity, ask yourself:

☆ "Why am I doing this?"
☆ "What do I hope to achieve?"
☆ "How does this fit in with my overall objectives?"
☆ "How will it take me closer to my goals?"

16. Don't be Superman or the Bionic Woman.

Few of us can do all things well. Therefore, don't attempt to master every aspect of your job. If you can rely on someone on your internal team or you can hire someone who can do it better, faster, or smarter—let them do it. Never attempt to perfect mediocrity.

17. Define your objectives and time frame.

Before meeting with your staff, clients, or prospects, establish the objectives of the meeting and how long it should take. I often ask clients, "How much time would you like to block for our discussion?" This simple question lets them know I respect their time and mine.

18. Prioritize.

Aside from just listing what needs to be done on your "to do" list, rank or prioritize your tasks. Then attack and complete them in that order.

19. Chart your day.

This suggestion sounds time-consuming. It is! However, if you divide your day into 10- or 15-minute time segments and record how you spend each segment, your findings might startle you.

For example, let's say you discover almost 30 minutes of each day is devoted to getting coffee, chitchatting, hanging at the watercooler, reviewing the big game last night, or other unproductive stuff.

Now I realize being friendly and social aren't bad qualities, but if you reduce the preceding activities to only 15 minutes, what's the significance?

Significant!

If you work only eight hours a day, 15 minutes represents 3 percent of your day. And when you squeeze an extra 15 minutes of productivity into every five-day workweek, that's 1.25 hours per week. Over a year, 1.25 hours of additional productivity time per week adds up to almost 63 hours of newly found selling time. That time will put dollars in your pocket!

20. Make phone appointments.

Avoid telephone tag. Instead, take a proactive step. I'll often ask a secretary, "How does Bob's schedule look tomorrow? . . . Really, that's great. Then let's plan a telephone date or appointment for 10:15. Please let Bob know that at exactly 10:15 tomorrow morning, I'll call him. . . . Wonderful. Thanks again for your help." The following day, at exactly 10:15 A.M., Bob's phone will ring!

On my desk I have a small clock that's especially helpful for when I make telephone dates with clients or prospects. Let's say I have a phone meeting scheduled for 10:15 A.M. At 10:12 the clock's alarm starts chiming.

This alerts me to stop another activity and to simply take out the notes, questions, and objectives I prepared for this call. Then, I start dialing. (The alarm clock assures I'm always on time or a wee bit early.) Others always know that if we set a telephone date, I'm punctual.

When the phone rings at 10:14 A.M., and if it's not answered by my client or prospect, I say to the secretary or receptionist something like:

☆ "Hi, this is Jeff Blackman for Bob. He's expecting my call at 10:15."

☆ "Hi, this is Jeff Blackman. Bob and I have a telephone meeting scheduled for 10:15 this morning. Could you please tell him I'm calling?"

The preceding greetings are polite and efficient. They also convey a sense of urgency or commitment.

I also use the same appointment strategy with clients and prospects, by simply leaving them a voice mail or e-mail message with two or three date and time possibilities for our next conversation. This enables them to pick the time that's best for their schedule and simply confirm it with me, via phone or e-mail. This strategy is quick. Convenient. Results-oriented. And it works.

21. Know the value of urgency.

Here's one more strategy to avoid the ongoing frustration of telephone tag. If you don't want to leave a message or attempt to set up a phone date, simply make this polite request of a secretary or receptionist: "Paige, I could sure use your help. Taylor and I have been chasing each other. Where can we please locate her now?!"

On a regular basis, people will say things like:

☆ "I'll go into her office and leave her a note right now."
☆ "I know where she's at; let me find her."
☆ "Let me page her!"
☆ "She told me you'd be calling; let me go get her!"

Others love to help. Give them the opportunity!

Management expert Peter Drucker once declared, "Time is the scarcest resource." Time really isn't scarce; it's uniform and constant. However, your ability to use it is crucial to your success. For without time management or self-management, you need not worry about cash management.

Profit Point

99

To know me is to love me.

"Organizing is what you do before you do something, so that when you do it, it's not all mixed up."

—*Christopher Robin in A. A. Milne's* Winnie the Pooh

To maximize your self-management, the following ideas, quotations, questions, and suggestions were created to help you, like they've helped me and countless others. Here's to your triumph of time and self!

Please circle yes or no for the following 46 questions:

1. **Are you in control of your environment?**
   Yes   No

2. **Do you effectively plan your travel time?**
   Yes   No

3. **Do you quickly and efficiently handle your paperwork?**
   Yes   No

4. **Do you have the time to prospect regularly and consistently?**
   Yes   No

5. **Is your income commensurate to your potential?**
   Yes   No

6. **Are you prepared mentally for each call or appointment?**
Yes   No

7. **Are you prepared physically for each call or appointment?**
Yes   No

8. **Do you normally arrive on time or early?**
Yes   No

9. **Do you have a goal or objective for each call?**
Yes   No

10. **Do you initiate or return phone calls on time?**
Yes   No

11. **Are you a better "time manager" now than one year ago?**
Yes   No

"Your choice...victim or victor!"

12. **Do you establish a "time agenda" with a customer or prospect before a meeting?**
Yes   No

13. **Do you have quarterly sales goals?**
Yes   No

14. **Do you have quarterly income goals?**
Yes   No

15. **When with a prospect or customer, do you concentrate on their needs versus what you left behind, your long "to do" list or your immediate crisis?**
Yes   No

16. **Do you ever "make a date with yourself" to creatively prioritize and strategize?**
Yes   No

17. **When waiting/holding on the telephone, do you have stuff to do (reading, reviewing mail, etc.)?**
Yes   No

18. Are your customers categorized by profitability, volume, or potential?

    Yes   No

19. Do you ask for referrals on a consistent basis?

    Yes   No

20. Do you invest in your ongoing education (reading books, attending courses, listening to tapes/CDs, etc.)?

    Yes   No

21. Do you have a stack of newspapers, magazines, or newsletters resembling Mount Everest?

    Yes   No

22. Do you have time to correspond with customers?

    Yes   No

> "Plan ahead, anticipate challenges . . .
> prepare solutions."

23. Have you developed a list of targeted or top priority customers for future business?

    Yes   No

24. Have you carefully examined your "portfolio" or "book of business" to best determine how to optimize results?

    Yes   No

25. Do you have a process or an organized approach to staying in touch with customers and prospects?

    Yes   No

26. Have you ever exclaimed, "Why does management send me all this junk!?"

    Yes   No

27. Do you limit your availability?

    Yes   No

28. Do you concentrate your phone calls?

    Yes   No

29. **Do you confirm appointments via phone or e-mail?**
    Yes   No

30. **Do you plan your day the night before?**
    Yes   No

31. **Do you use a cellular phone to improve your productivity?**
    Yes   No

32. **Do you standardize your letters and e-mails?**
    Yes   No

33. **When you plan your "to do" list, do you allot the amount of time each activity should take?**
    Yes   No

> **"At about 4:45 P.M., you must decide . . .**
> **are you tired or lazy?!"**

34. **Do you listen to cassettes or CDs while exercising or driving?**
    Yes   No

35. **Do you make time for personal activities or hobbies?**
    Yes   No

36. **Do you make time to exercise on a regular basis?**
    Yes   No

37. **Are your professional goals written down and prioritized with due dates?**
    Yes   No

38. **Are your personal goals written down and prioritized with due dates?**
    Yes   No

39. **Do you have a written list featuring at least 12 power probes or open-ended need-development questions, plus at least two open-ended referral-seeking questions?**
    Yes   No

40. Are you working as smart as you can?
Yes   No

41. Do you have a written list of your most commonly heard objections, obstacles, or decision delayers, and most important, the language you would use to overcome them?
Yes   No

42. Do you initiate or return e-mails on time?
Yes   No

43. Do you devote time each day to surf the Web—to learn more about your industry, competition, trends, business, and life *or* to read a book on the best-seller list, a magazine related to your industry, a publication that has nothing to do with your business, or a local or national newspaper?
Yes   No

44. Do you make time for family activities?
Yes   No

45. Do your actions speak louder than your words?
Yes   No

46. At some point in this century, will the Chicago Cubs, Sox, Bears, Bulls, or Blackhawks win a championship?
Yes   No

As a result of your answers to the preceding questions:

What have you learned about yourself?
What surprised you?
What obstacles are standing in your way?
Where are there opportunities for improvement?
What will you do differently?
When will you take action?

Profit Point

100

Focus Five.

Procrastination is your foe.
Indecision an assassin.
Make every day count.

"The time for action is now. It's never too late to do some-thing."

—*Carl Sandburg*

Time for another gut-check question:

What haven't *you* done that
if *you* did . . .
would significantly change and upgrade
how *you* do business?

Now, create your Focus Five. It's your commitment to actionable, quantifiable, measurable behaviors and results for a week, a month, a quarter, or a year. Your Focus Five specifies the activities you'll focus on in order to achieve your goals.

My Focus Five

1. _____

_____

_____

_____

2. _____

_____

_____

_____

3. _____

_____

_____

_____

4. _____

_____

_____

_____

5. _____

_____

_____

_____

Make your Focus Five.
Commit to it.
Make it happen.

P.I.T. Stop

P   Provocative or Playful

I   Inspirational or Informational

T   Thoughts or Theories

"What we learn after we know it all is what counts!"

"My therapist told me that the way to achieve true inner peace is to finish what I start. So far today, I have finished two bags of chips and a chocolate cake. I feel better already."
> —My sister, Tammie Blackman Brown

"It gets late early out here."
> —Yogi Berra

"You know you're getting older when you have two temptations for the evening . . . and you choose the one that gets you home by nine!"
> —My friend Mike Wynne

"Waiting is a trap. There will always be reasons to wait. The truth is, there are only two things in life, reasons and results, and reasons simply don't count."
> —Robert Anthony

Final Stuff

Now what?

That's up to you!

Yet if you're like my other clients, who are achieving
meteoric results—as they successfully travel
to that special place known as
"the next level"—you, too, now know . . .
it's time to turn . . .

Ideas into implementation.

Knowledge into action.

Principles into results.

And strategies into sales.

Go execute.

Deliver value.

Help others attain a more favorable future.

Make it happen.

Now!

And please tell me all about your stories of success
and tales of triumph.

E-mail me at jeff@jeffblackman.com
or buzz me at (847) 998-0688.

My goal is to help you meet and exceed your goals!

For winners possess a common quality, and that's focus—
to turn fantasy into fact and dreams into reality.

Embrace your dreams!

Meet Jeff Blackman

Jeff is a speaker, author, success coach, broadcast personality, and lawyer. He heads Blackman & Associates, a creative and results-producing business-growth firm in the Chicago area. His clients call him a "business-growth specialist." For example, Jeff's customized "Referrals: Your Road to Results" learning system helped Banc One generate $230 million in new business directly from referrals, in only 23 months.

For over two decades, Jeff has shared his positive and profit-producing messages with numerous Fortune 500 companies, closely held businesses, entrepreneurial organizations, and association audiences throughout the world.

As a radio and TV talk-show host, some of Jeff's guests have been Oprah Winfrey, Ted Koppel, Jerry Seinfeld, Marcel Marceau, astronaut Jim Lovell, and Olympic gold medalists Bruce Jenner and Dan Jansen.

Jeff is a contributing editor to numerous magazines and newspapers. His other books and audio and video growth tools include:

☆ *Peak Your Profits.*

☆ *Opportunity $elling.*

☆ *RESULT$: Proven Sales Strategies for Changing Times.*

☆ *Carpe A.M., Carpe P.M.—Seize Your Destiny!*

☆ *Opportunity $elling—Six Profit-Producing Steps to Multiply Your Earnings.*

☆ *Profitable Customer Service.*

☆ *How to Set and Really Achieve Your Goals.*

Jeff is also a member of the National Speakers Association (NSA) and one of less than 10 percent of professional speakers to receive the coveted Certified Speaking Professional (CSP) designation from NSA.

Jeff graduated with honors from both the University of Illinois and the Illinois Institute of Technology Chicago Kent College of Law. He's also a happy husband, devoted father, avid softball player, and loyal but often depressed Chicago Cubs fan!

Jeff Blackman helps you *create profits through people!*

Jeff educates, entertains, and inspires!

Whether giving an intimate workshop for 30 or a dynamic keynote presentation for thousands, when Jeff speaks—he educates, entertains, and inspires!

Hire speakers for your company? Influence the selection of speakers at your industry association? Hire Jeff! He . . .

☆ Delivers proven strategies on sales, negotiations, marketing, referrals, service, inspiration, leadership, and change—to create lifelong opportunities for growth and prosperity.

☆ Motivates you to meet and exceed your goals.

☆ Turns new knowledge and skills into power and profit.

☆ Energizes you to discover passion, purpose, and fun.

☆ Shows you how to hurdle your belief barriers.

☆ Creates an atmosphere for meaningful action . . . resulting in a lifetime of significant achievement.

What do clients value most about Jeff's speaking engagements, training programs, workshops, consultations, and ongoing learning systems? His . . .

☆ Energy and quick connection with an audience.

☆ Quality content and real-world solutions.

☆ Warm, friendly, and impactful style.

☆ Commitment to customization and exhaustive research.

☆ Powerful profit-producing messages.

☆ Sense of humor and spontaneity—you laugh while you learn.

☆ Meaningful and fun audience interaction.

☆ Focus on quantifiable results and outcomes—for the long term.

Please contact Jeff to yak about biz, baseball, and how he'll help you grow, prosper, and win!

Blackman & Associates, Inc.
Creating Profits Through People
2130 Warwick Lane, Glenview, IL 60025
Phone: (847) 998-0688 • Fax: (847) 998-0675
jeff@jeffblackman.com or jbresults@aol.com
**visit www.jeffblackman.com and
subscribe to Jeff's *free* Results Report**

Jeff's growth tools accelerate your career, grow your business, and improve your life!

Since you're serious about success—Jeff's growth tools are a must for your learning library or as a gift for someone else.

To preview these growth tools, read excerpts, or order them, please log on to www.jeffblackman.com and simply click on Growth Tools. Or call (847) 998-0688.

Special thanks to . . .

My wife, Sheryl . . .

You're my "date for life"! After 21 years of marriage, you remain my light, love, and laughter. Thanks for all you are and all you do. And for worrying about everything, so I can worry about nothing. I love you! Even if you remind me to take out the garbage on Sunday nights!

My kids: Chad, Brittany, and Amanda . . .

Who now realize—between car pools, baseball games, drum lessons, tennis lessons, dance recitals, ice shows, choir and band performances, school and religious activities . . . Daddy works! Each of you is special. And Daddy loves you more than you'll ever know.

Mom and Dad . . .

a.k.a. "Irv and Sal" or "Mama and Papa." Thanks for teaching me at a young age the importance of integrity and to always try to do the right thing. Hope you're proud of your "JB Boy" because I'm sure proud of you. I love you!

Dad . . .

To lots of the world, you're Irv Blackman, CPA, lawyer, bank chairman, board member, financial adviser. To me, you're Dad or Pop! Thanks for still being the best mentor a little boy could ever have.

My in-laws . . .

Beverly and Leo Kantor, who still aren't quite sure what I do for a living, but they're glad I do it. I love you!

My clients . . .

Who inspire and challenge me. You make it all worthwhile: the travel, the long hours, the problem solving, the creative solutions, the what-ifs, the "wouldn't it be cool if" possibilities, and most important . . . the results! My greatest satisfaction is to hear the excitement in your voices when you exclaim, "It works! Big time!" If you're already a client, you know what to expect and how much you're valued. And if you're a future client, we'll prove to you just how much we're worth.

My friends and family . . .

For your encouragement, support, and love. The journey is a heckuva lot easier with all of you at my side—whether we're eating, laughing, eating, crying, eating, talking, eating, or playing. Have I mentioned eating?

My NSA buddies . . .

For being some of the smartest, nuttiest, and most gracious folks I know. The National Speakers Association has given me a dynamic network of friends and advisers. There are literally hundreds of NSAers who have positively influenced my life and career. To each, I'm eternally grateful.

All the folks who read my
newspaper and magazine columns . . .

Although we may never meet, it's a pleasure and privilege to capture your eyeballs. Your kind words, insightful questions, and valuable ideas motivate me to write each column and then the next one. (If you'd like me to write for your industry publication or local business paper, please give me a holler so we can explore the possibilities.)

The worldwide audience who reads my free e-letter,
The Results Report . . .

It began with a simple concept and a few hundred "subscribers" in February 2000. Now, it's read by thousands in 42 countries. The greatest compliments are when you tell me how you applied a strategy that's now delivering results and when you add to the distribution list your clients, customers, prospects, friends, peers, and family. Thank you!

My "contributing consultants" . . .

John Alston, Steve Attenberg, Major Avignon, Alan Brown, Larry S. Brown, Connie Bruno, Frank Bucaro, Bob Burg, Joe Calloway, Todd Carlson, Steve Casper, Ed Chesen, Marlene Chism, Jim Clark, Pat Constabileo, Alan Cruise, Jeffrey Davis, Yvonne Dean, Jeff Eskow, Anne Fawley, Christine Federico, Diane Fontenot, Martin Ginsburg, Jeffrey Gitomer, Andrea Gold, Richard Harrington, Michelle Harris, Jason Robert Isenga, Dr. Philip Ernest Johnson, Mike Kalnitz, Jason Kinney, Donavan J. Lopez, Mac McAllister, Jim Meisenheimer, Wayne Messmer, Marilynn Mobley, Erl Morrell-Stinson, Bruce Neumann, Charles Ng, Hai T. Nguyen, Lynn O'Connor, Mark Paape, Michelle Petro, Mike Phillips, Brent Ritchie, Tom Rosendahl, Steve Rubin, John Setlak, Jerry Shapiro, Marc Sher, Brad Skuran, Steven W. Smith, Ron Springer, Robert J. Stalvey, Lori Buss Stillman, Gary P. Stone, Roz Usheroff, Ed Walovitch, Alan Weiss, and Kevin Zylka.

Each of you, in some way, influenced the book's title, subtitle, content, and birth. Thanks for your counsel and candor.

Matt Holt, Senior Editor at John Wiley & Sons . . .

From our first conversation, I sensed Matt, Wiley, and myself would give birth to a blockbuster book. My intuition was right.

Matt, thanks for making it so easy. I especially appreciate your enthusiastic support, sage advice, and good-natured ribbing.

Michelle Becker, Tamara Hummel, Linda Indig, and . . .

The rest of the gang at John Wiley & Sons.

My copy editors . . .

The nice folks at Cape Cod Compositors who know all the fancy grammar rules that I ignore. Without you, it ain't a book!

Angela Graham . . .

My high school English teacher, for teaching me to love and value the written word. And for being in my audience at a book signing, 22 years after you graded my final exam!

Donna Northrup . . .

My first grade teacher, who didn't laugh when she first heard me speak. Instead, she cheerfully encouraged me to attend my daily speech cuh-weck-shun wessons. Little did she realize she was shaping my life and career.

The Chicago Cubs . . .

As a diehard fan who bleeds Cubbie blue, you've taught me to always believe, dream, and imagine the possibilities—even though you keep finding ways to rip my heart out! While any team can have a bad century, let's hope the 21st isn't another one!

And thanks to you . . .

For investing in me.

For investing in this book.

And most important, for investing in yourself.

Start selling! Keep winning!

Index